*How to*
## RAISE
-*a*-
## READER

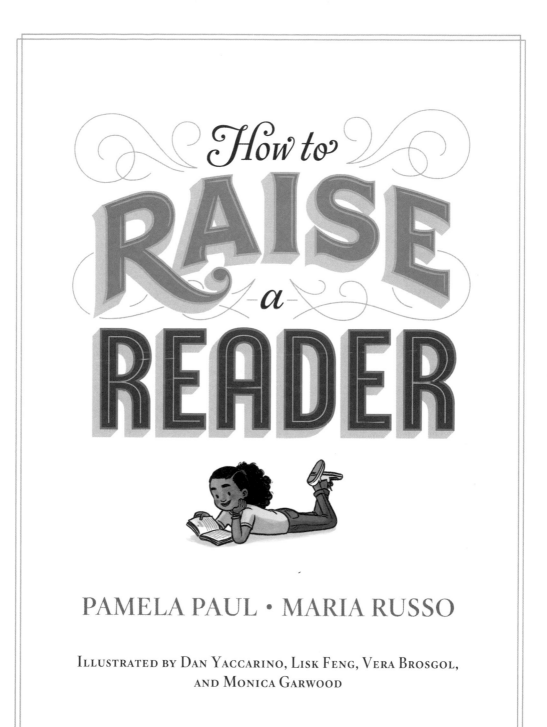

# How to RAISE a READER

## PAMELA PAUL · MARIA RUSSO

ILLUSTRATED BY DAN YACCARINO, LISK FENG, VERA BROSGOL,
AND MONICA GARWOOD

WORKMAN PUBLISHING · NEW YORK

# Dedication

FROM PAMELA
FOR BEATRICE, TOBIAS, AND THEODORE, MY READERS

FROM MARIA
FOR AUGUST LARKIN, MARIO JAMES, AND DANTE NICHOLAS

Library of Congress Cataloging-in-Publication Data is available.

ISBN 978-1-5235-0530-2

Art direction by Janet Vicario
Cover art by Jessica Hische

Workman books are available at special discounts when purchased in bulk for premiums and sales promotions as well as for fund-raising or educational use. Special editions or book excerpts can also be created to specification. For details, contact the Special Sales Director at the address below, or send an email to specialmarkets@workman.com.

Workman Publishing Co., Inc.
225 Varick Street
New York, NY 10014-4381

workman.com

WORKMAN is a registered trademark of Workman Publishing Co., Inc.

Printed in China
First printing July 2019

10 9 8 7 6 5 4 3 2 1

# CONTENTS

# INTRODUCTION

Do you remember what it was like as a child to get lost in a story? The way the world around you dropped away, except perhaps for the musty smell of a good book or the warm presence of your father on the beanbag chair next to you? Maybe you once hid out in the stacks of the local library, immersed in the first Harry Potter novel, desperately turning the pages to find out the meaning of the Sorcerer's Stone. Or maybe you can recall being curled up in your mother's lap, imagining what it would be like to eat all the berries you could on Blueberry Hill. Do you remember your first visit to where the wild things are? Did you think that maybe you could somehow one day go there yourself?

Whatever image jumps to mind, it's probably rich with pleasurable associations: a child—you—experiencing the comfort and fascination of a private world, the joy of total absorption in an activity, the bliss of feeling like time has stopped.

Now that you're an adult watching the next generation of kids grow up, does it sometimes feel like that sensation of lost time has itself been lost? Or like it might be harder for kids today to find those empty pockets of time, to be able to dive headlong into a book? Is reading for pleasure still the carefree pastime it once was, as much a part of the timeline of growing up as climbing a tree or learning to ride a bike? Chances are, if you're picking up a book like this, you want your child to experience all the natural, timeless, time-stopping joys of reading. You care about your child's relationship to books and want to be sure the written word becomes an integral part of her formative years. But you wish there were some greater support system around raising a reader.

Even as someone committed to fostering your child's reading, you may still sometimes feel some nagging worries around it. They may in fact all be in your own head, but that doesn't make them feel any less powerful. The stress often begins when the child is still fiddling with refrigerator alphabet letters and marveling at the letters shown on the screen during an educational cartoon. Well before school even begins, a parent's concern about "measuring up" might kick in: Why hasn't my child mastered the alphabet yet? And from there it can spiral: Is my child reading soon enough, fast enough, in an advanced enough way? It can head into some pretty dire territory: Will he get into a good college, get a good job, become economically self-sufficient? Then, of course, there's that growing fear for the future of humanity: Will the next generation even read books at all or will they spend the hours robotically scrolling down on electronic devices, as helpless and co-opted as players at a casino slot machine? Will our own children be contributing to that apocalyptic vision? (Don't worry; the answer is no.)

Amid all this, it can seem hard to conjure up simple, happy images of kids with books, reading in some pure, unpressured way, just for the joy of it. But that is the starting point of this book. Keep those pictures in mind as your beacons, because it turns out that many of the life goals we have for our children flow naturally out of the experience of reading for pleasure when they're young.

Children who read are, yes, likely to excel academically, but there's much more to the picture. The latest research shows that children who read at home are also better at self-regulation and executive function—those life skills that make us happier and well adjusted: controlling impulses, paying attention, setting goals and figuring out how to achieve them. Think of this as "life readiness." By being part of your child's reading life—by setting out purposefully to raise a reader—you're helping her become someone who controls her own destiny.

School is where children learn that they *have* to read. Home is where kids learn to read because they *want* to. It's where they learn to *love* to read. It's always amazing to register the difference when a child freely chooses any activity. Somehow, her mood is lighter. A sense of purpose seems to emanate from a genuine, happy place. There's a palpable eagerness rather than a foot-dragging reticence. So let's think about the long-term project of raising a reader not as an obligation but as an opportunity to bring some wonderful things into your child's and your family's life. The parent's part in encouraging a reader is in many ways more interesting, joyful, and open-ended than the school's part of the project, which is focused on things like phonics, assessments, and benchmarks.

Our hope is that this book serves as comfort, validation, and inspiration, not only for you as a parent but for your own life as a reader as well. We want to help nurture the love and appreciation of books and literature that you already feel, whether it was instilled in you during childhood or developed later on. We want this book to be useful to you but also to be fun, just as reading is fun. For our part, we had a great time gathering our best tips and ideas and, especially, our favorite book recommendations. As parents of three children each, and as people who work with books every day (yes, we realize how lucky we are), we've been steeped in children's literature for years.

Whether you pick up this book as an expecting parent, an experienced parent, a grandparent, a teacher, or a concerned caregiver, we like to think you'll come away from it with ideas, inspiration, encouragement, and, possibly, relief. Our hope is that you'll find yourself seeking it out again and again, whether for reassurance or a reminder, or to move on to the next section as your child moves to the next stage in her reading life. Our greatest hope is that one day, one of your children will pick it up and leaf through it with recognition and gratitude. Perhaps they'll want to keep it for themselves to share with their own children. We all love remembering the satisfaction, the joy, the almost giddy exhilaration of seeing the world of letters, and as a consequence the entire world, open up to us.

### A Note from Maria

A memory: I'm sitting up in my 6-year-old son's captain's bed between him and his 8½-year-old sister. "'It's a Sea-Serpent! It's a Prock! It's a Manticore!'" I read. They both begin laughing out loud. I forge on as James Henry Trotter and his insect friends frighten New York City from their giant peach, spiked atop the Empire State Building: "'That one's an Oinck!' screamed the Head of the Fire Department. 'I just *know* it's an Oinck.'" At that point I stop and the three of us say, "I just *know* it's an Oinck" over and over, between waves of laughter.

The copy of Roald Dahl's *James and the Giant Peach* that I read to them, and later to their younger brother, came from my own childhood, a gift to 7-year-old me from a family friend. The dust jacket is long gone, but the sight of its faded orange cloth cover can send me straight back to the feeling of being a child myself, reading about poor, lucky James and his terrible, thrilling adventure. The story's details feel lodged in my very being. I consider it incredibly good fortune that I got to return to it as a parent and share it with my children. You could say it's love itself that shines out of those memories.

It's stressful to be a parent. It's stressful to be a *person*. But I've found that even in the most difficult moments, on the most challenging days, I can usually reach for a book and feel lifted up, returned to myself. On days when I've felt as though I have nothing left to give to my kids, I've been able to sit next to them and open a book. We start reading, and the world looks different.

Sometimes when my mind starts flailing into some worry about my kids' current or future struggles, about whether my husband and I have taken this or that right path with them, I remind myself that every book they've read or had read to them has left behind some trace, some potential memory, and that those memories build on themselves and lead to other good things. For me the proof is in my experience with *James and the Giant Peach*.

When my children were 11, 8, and 3, our lives changed after we moved from California to New York and I took a job as the children's books editor at the *New York Times*. More books started flowing in and out of our home. My children became my test crew, a role they've loved and, at times, resented or outright refused. Maybe the most satisfying stories of their reading lives have nothing to do with me: a teacher pulling me aside to let me know that my daughter had been weeping while she read *The Book Thief* during the class's silent reading period that day, or the first time my oldest son carried a book—Jeff Smith's *Bone*—with him everywhere, reading in the car and in restaurants and in a doctor's waiting room, or my younger son's shouts of excitement in second grade when the books he'd chosen from his school's book fair finally arrived.

Likewise, my deeper dive into the world of children's books has been a daily joy, but it has come with its own challenges. I sort through children's books for what sometimes feels like endless stretches, putting some onto shelves and pulling others off until my shoulders ache and my eyes cross. How can there possibly be so many? How can I do justice to them all? But then it happens: I open a box to find a stack of Sandra Boynton board books, and I can picture vividly my daughter as a toddler nestled in my lap on a purple beanbag chair as I read, for the hundredth time, "'A cow says moo, a sheep says baa, three singing pigs say . . .'" and my daughter shouts, "'La la la!'"

"A minute spent reading to your kids now will repay itself a million-fold later," the author George Saunders once wrote, "not only because they love you for reading to them, but also because, years later, when they're miles away, those quiet evenings when you were tucked in with them, everything quiet but the sound of the page-turns, will seem to you, I promise, sacred." Raising a family of readers is a rewarding, never-ending voyage, and I hope this book will help you and the children in your life construct your own personalized itinerary for it.

## A Note from Pamela

I was one of those kids who always had her nose in a book, something that wasn't always viewed as a capital achievement back when I was growing up. A shy child who failed to excel at music, art, or sports, I felt more at home in stories. Life inside a book often seemed better to me than life out there, which felt full of threat, often without helpful foreshadowing. Little did I realize at the time that those books would help equip me with the knowledge and skills I needed once I mustered the courage to venture outside; they helped me learn to take risks. Reading for me has been a lifelong lifeline.

It's not surprising, then, that for me, writing a book about raising readers is a labor of love, bringing together four things close to my heart: children, books, education, and parenthood—and for me, those four things are bound together. Even my visions of parenthood were informed by reading. I'm one of those people who always knew she wanted children, the more the merrier. When I think back on this dream, I recognize its roots in the books I loved as a child—the All-of-a-Kind Family books, *Little Women, Cheaper by the Dozen.*

Not surprisingly, many of my fantasies around abundant motherhood centered on shared storytelling, the snuggling in at bedtime with *Through the Looking-Glass.* Cozy gatherings by the fireplace, its flickering light casting a glow on the page. Ghost stories whispered aloud by flashlight.

I looked forward to sharing the stories I loved with my children and to discovering new ones through them.

I always knew my children would read—or at least, I never stopped to entertain the notion that they might not. Though I know children are different from their parents (and mine certainly are), it seemed impossible to me that they wouldn't take part in these family scenes. Even if on a practical level, it was unimaginable: What would I do, then, with all the children's books I'd saved from my own childhood (battered copies of *A Light in the Attic* and the collected Frances Hodgson Burnett)? Or the Dr. Seuss classics I'd purchased on sale in hardcover when I was in my twenties, and still entirely single and years away from parenthood.

Happily, buying those books and saving my old copies wasn't for naught. Plenty of parents can show off with good reason about their kids' strengths and skills. And certainly my children aren't perfect or good at everything. But I can say that all three of them, now between the ages of 9 and 13, are enthusiastic readers. They are, in fact, far better readers than I am—more adventurous than I was at their age, better rereaders, and more voracious. They tend to look on their poor mother as woefully slow and distracted. "What page are you still on?!" they ask as I slowly and distractedly gaze at my book after a long day.

I'm okay with that. I am okay with the fact that they turn the pages more quickly than I do and ignore me occasionally when I call them to dinner because they want to finish a chapter. I am more than okay with knowing that whatever life out there holds for them, they will be more ready for it, having indulged in the stories held within books. They will understand story line and plot twists and happy endings. They will know about character development and underlying themes and sad endings as well. Through the novels they've read, they will know more about the stories they want to be a part of, what kind of character they might be. They'll be better prepared to read situations and to understand context and to search for meaning in the face of the seemingly incomprehensible. They will know how to break a story down to its essential elements and draw conclusions. They will be able to read people and situate themselves and others in the world. My hope is that they will seize on books as their own lifelines and share their stories with others.

# PART ONE

# Born to Read

*We've divided this first part,
about babies and toddlers, into two sections.
The precious time between parent, baby,
and book is the very beginning of a reader's
life story. The leap to toddlerhood thickens the
plot considerably. So we are devoting several pages
and lots of book suggestions to each stage.*

# READING TO YOUR BABY

Maybe you're in those heady first few months of parenthood, or maybe you're still waiting for your baby to arrive. In either case: Congratulations! You're here to think about your child's reading, but let's start with your own. . . . It's likely you've recently perused at least one book about pregnancy and childbirth, and another about newborn care, both of which are important. But here is our first recommendation for raising a reader: Before your child even arrives, and in those jam-packed newborn days, spend some time with at least one book you love that's not about any of that practical stuff. It can be an old book or a new one, something you first read years ago or a current bestseller. It can be fiction or history or poetry or memoir. It can be funny or sad, a graphic novel or a manifesto about gardening. Just open it and relax into it. Reading is an especially good way to connect to your own inner life, and now is a great time to do exactly that. Who you are and the way you live are about to matter in a whole new way. You're creating—or expanding—a family and a family culture. A little human is going to be paying attention to you, absorbing the signals you send about how to live, what counts most, and what cultures and ideas you think are valuable.

Right now, how do you spend your free time? How do you pass the hours—or the spare minutes? We all have a lot pulling at our attention these days. If you've let reading slide to the margins of your life, now is the time to gently bring it back toward the center. Books are a pleasure and they anchor your greater values. So make the space and the time for books you read for yourself.

It comes down to this: **If you want to raise a reader, *be* a reader.**

## Here's What You Need to Know

### Babies Really Do Need Books

Read to your baby. You've probably heard that from multiple sources by now, from your pediatrician to your mother-in-law to the woman behind you in the supermarket checkout line. They're right, of course, but let's face it—it can feel a bit ridiculous to read to a baby. Here you are, trilling aloud in a sing-songy voice, describing a story about a duck and goose with full-on feeling, and your baby can't even see across the room clearly yet, never mind see the words on the page.

Reading to a newborn may seem like reading to yourself for all the reaction you get. Newborns are squirmy. They can't focus their eyes. They fall asleep. The back-and-forth that can make a read-aloud session so satisfying to all involved just isn't going to happen at first. It's not until they're about 3 months old that most babies start to seem more aware of being read to. That's a fine time to start reading to them, but if you can work some reading into your days earlier, go for it. The sound of your voice is what counts from day one. The words themselves. The cadence of the sentences. The comfort and connection of being held or sitting close. The pleasure of being paid attention to. Their sense of your own pleasure.

### The Book Doesn't Always Matter

Right away, you can start reading board books and picture books to an infant—the books that will become part of his library. But any book is good. If you're so inclined, you can also read him a cookbook, a novel, a parenting manual—anything constructed of words. Research shows that the number of words an infant is exposed to has a direct effect on language development and literacy, whether they understand them immediately or not. Many of us know this instinctively; it's why we find ourselves incessantly babbling away while changing a diaper. But here's the catch to language exposure: Those words have to be live, in person, and directed at the child. Turning on a video, or even an audiobook, doesn't count. This is about *you* reading aloud to them.

Whatever you're reading, make it an enjoyable moment. If you're inspired, use silly voices. Sing the words. Feel no compunction about using words your infant doesn't yet understand. If you're really into your own book, read a paragraph aloud here and there while your baby is in tummy-time mode or nursing. This needn't—and shouldn't—be exhausting. Babies pick up on our emotions and tone more than the content itself, so do it when you're feeling inspired. Sometimes it's just the thing to keep yourself awake and feeling a part of the world in those early days with a newborn.

## Full-Body Reading

Babies who are read to are learning not only that reading is fun but also that reading can involve all the senses: not just the sound of the parent's voice but also, eventually, the feel of the pages, the shape and weight of the book, the smell of the glue (don't go crazy), the visuals of the illustrations. In the first few months of life, babies' eyes wander as they're being read to, but by 7 to 10 months, they are usually able to pick up on the visual aspect of a book. Point to those pictures she shows an interest in and tell her more about them. Remember: At this point, you don't need to be wedded to the particular words that are on the page.

Even earlier than that, though—perhaps even from 2 months old—she can get involved in the process in a tactile way. Help her touch the pages with her hands. More and more books for infants are textured on some or all of their pages, which is especially good for your baby's developing experience of touch. Show her what there is to feel and let her feel it.

### Don't Expect Obvious Interaction

When you read to a baby, don't look for any particular reaction. A day will come when a little more of a back-and-forth rhythm develops between you. Your baby may start making sounds in response to your reading. This is why many books for babies contain nonsense words or animal sounds — they're easier to mimic. When your child makes a noise that sounds purposeful, respond in words or in your own nonsense sounds. It may make no obvious sense, but it's communication. Some books, such as those with animal noises or told through dialogue, beg for a call-and-response, even if that response is merely a gurgle. There's a straight line from this inchoate moment to your first parent-child book club.

### Book Culture

Be aware that beyond just reading to your baby, what you're doing in that first year is introducing her to the culture of reading in the broadest possible sense. Having books in her daily life — strewn about her crib and on her play mat, standing up on a shelf she can see, stacked on a table — tells her that reading is a natural and valuable part of her world. Having special books read at a certain time of day conveys that books are part of the comforting and predictable routines from which days are made. Having someone take the time to read to him, and when appropriate, ask for his attention, sets the stage for the more formalized learning that will be part of his life as he grows. To have someone remember a favorite book and sit down to read it aloud is, quite simply, to feel loved.

### Those Old-Timey Classics

Most parents tend to start with the books they loved when they were little, and that's a great place to begin. After all, you already love the books, and it's deliciously nostalgic to revisit them. (*The Story of Ferdinand*!) Because so many parents turn to their own childhood favorites first, great children's books tend to stay in print for a long time, often in inexpensive paperbacks. These backlist books are a staple of children's publishing and continue to outsell most new children's books. Of course, not all your favorites may still be in print. Some you may need to hunt down online or in used bookstores. For Pamela, the discovery of Purple House Press, a website that sells classics that had previously gone out of print, was especially exciting.

But you may notice some startlingly antiquated text or images in those great classics. The little girls in those charming Golden Books stories from the forties may be invariably blond and pinafored. They all want to be nurses while their brothers aspire to be doctors. Where are all the brown- and black-skinned kids, and why is Christmas the only holiday? Many classic children's books are now considered sexist, racist, outdated, and, in certain ways, downright awful. Kids are occasionally referred to as "stupid." Children treat one another in bullying ways that would nowadays land them swiftly in the principal's office. Parents tell their children not to talk at the dinner table. Go ahead and make old books better, if you can (some, alas, are irredeemable). Feel free to tweak the text when you're reading out loud. Edit them as you narrate; especially at this early stage, your child won't notice, and you can give them the good parts and leave out the bad.

## What to Look For: Baby Books

### Go with Board Books

Board books are small, thick cardboard books that fit in a baby's hand and are aimed at babies, ages 0 to 3. They can be safely chewed on or thrown across the room. Like their bigger cousins, picture books, board books are visual and verbal; pictures tell the story as much as the words do, often more so. Many contain no words at all, which may feel like a "waste" of money, but we assure you, they are not. Board books can—and should—be simple and straightforward enough to hold a baby's attention.

### Familiarity

Our tiniest family members like to see their own world reflected on the page—including other babies' faces, and seemingly ho-hum household features like a stroller, a bathtub, or a crib. Because these books can feel boring to you, you may think they are boring to their intended reader. They are not. Remember that the world is new to a baby, so to see virtually

anything familiar in a book can bring the excitement of recognition. Look for board books that capture aspects of your baby's everyday life: people, animals, nature, homes, cars, cities. They are also learning that objects they see in the world around them can be represented in the pages of a book.

### A Simple Feast for the Eyes

Board books should have big, bright images and comparatively few words. For very small babies who can't yet focus well and don't perceive gradations of color, easy to see, simple black-and-white pages with big patterns are a great way to start. As your baby gets older, find board books with bold color combinations and high-impact graphic design. At this early stage, you're looking for loud and clear over soft and subtle.

### All Hands on Board

Once your child has good hand control, usually from about 4 months on, he can really get involved in the physical aspects of reading. Now is the time to lift the flap. Feel the textures. Pull the tabs. As soon as they can use their hands to make things happen, babies love to

manipulate these features of board books. For babies, this *is* reading. So make sure you have some lift-the-flap and texturized board books like the great Dorothy Kunhardt standbys *Pat the Bunny* and *The Telephone Book*. Priddy Books makes books with soft cloth pages and a Velcro fastener, a wonderful way to make reading a tactile activity as well as to introduce the element of surprise into story time.

### Go with Durability

Certain books are going to demand—and reward—frequent rereading, and for these, choose the board book over the paperback or the bigger hardcover picture book while your child is still a baby, and well into the toddler years. Young hands are going to grab and fondle and occasionally throw a book they love, so you want one that will resist tearing. If you think that a book is going to have to withstand years of abuse—say, Margaret Wise Brown's bedtime classic *Goodnight Moon*—get it in the board-book format, even if it's also available with bigger—rippable!—pages. (Trust us on the fate of this book if the pages are not sturdy.) For low-word-count, high-interaction stories, board books are the gold standard. Knowing how rough babies are on books, several publishers have come up with ingenious variations on the standard cardboard board book. The Indestructibles series, for example, can be taken in the bath or to the pool or beach without a second thought. Plastic "bath books" are built to go underwater, and because so many babies chew on books, they are made without dangerous chemicals you wouldn't want a small child ingesting along with his words.

# Be Wary Of

### A Lot of Blah-Blah-Blah or Visual Clutter

Too many words, and too many or too finely detailed pictures, will try a baby's patience. Every word and image in a board book should count. Think about it this way: Your baby is reading the pictures while you read the words; find books that make both of those experiences worthwhile.

### Board-Book Versions of All Your Favorites

Many picture books have been turned into board-book counterparts, which are tempting. But not every book that started out as a picture book works in a smaller, shorter format. Tiny, detailed drawings can get lost. There has to be a strong, simple visual component to the story. There may simply be too many words on the page. For many of your favorites, it may be best to wait until your baby morphs into a preschooler and can better experience that beloved book in its bigger, intended format.

### Gizmos and Battery-Powered Sounds

Babies get easily overstimulated, and they will also quickly tire of these bells and whistles. (You will, too.) You're also needlessly raising the stakes: Reading in and of itself is exciting. Your live, human voice should trump everything else. Skip the books with battery-operated buttons; it will also save you from a potential tantrum when the often-irreplaceable specialized batteries wear out.

# Our Baby Book Picks

## ALL-AROUND BEST BOARD BOOKS

### Look, Look!
**Peter Linenthal**

In the very first months of your baby's life, you want a black-and-white, high-contrast board book for her to look at, and this one has fascinating shapes—the sun, a hand—made with lovely paper-cut art, along with a few friendly, happy words.

### Where Is Baby's Belly Button?
**Karen Katz**

Babies love exploring their own bodies, and this peekaboo book, one of the great lift-the-flap books, allows them to do so actively. Katz's illustrations are adorable; seek out her many other interactive board books, too.

### MOO, BAA, LA LA LA! AND But Not the Hippopotamus
**Sandra Boynton**

Boynton is a one-woman institution in the books-for-tots universe, and these two are our favorites of her many books. Her ear for humor that tiny ones can understand is on impeccable display, and the words are delightfully easy to memorize.

### Mrs. Mustard's Baby Faces
**Jane Wattenberg**

There are a zillion board books about baby faces, but you want one like this adorably designed and racially diverse collection that includes photographs of real babies. Babies really like to look at other real babies. They like to look at their facial expressions, even when they're frowning or flooded in tears. Consider it early validation.

### Babies
**Gyo Fujikawa**

This "tall" board book is full of tender but humor-tinged drawings of round-cheeked babies of all races observed in infancy by older siblings until they reach toddlerhood.

### Color Zoo AND Color Farm
**Lois Ehlert**

The bright colors and bold shapes change into different animals very subtly, page by page, with cutouts for baby fingers to explore.

### Five Little Monkeys Jumping on the Bed
**Eileen Christelow**

The verse-like rhythms of this silly story read like a song and are often best accompanied by tickles and some live romping around. Do not expect it to lull little ones to sleep.

### Little Blue Truck
**Alice Schertle,**
**illustrated by Jill McElmurry**
This modern classic manages to get truck sounds—*beep*, *vroom*—and farm-animal sounds—*moo*, *oink*, and so on—into one story that rolls along in a satisfying way.

### My Car
**Byron Barton**
Loose lines, simple shapes, and primary colors accompany this easy story that unfolds as vehicles zip by. Other great titles in the "collection" are *Trains*, *Planes*, *Trucks*, and *My Bike*.

### No No Yes Yes
**Leslie Patricelli**
This book has only two words, but they are, of course, words your baby hears a lot, presented in Patricelli's characteristic bold, funny, visual style.

### Gossie
**Olivier Dunrea**
Gossie is a baby duck, and gosh is he cute. Along with a menagerie of friends, he tromps through stories about friendship, differences, sharing, and other pressing matters of early social life.

### Llama Llama Red Pajama
**Anna Dewdney**
All of Dewdney's popular Llama Llama books are extremely satisfying for toddlers, with their warm art, perfect rhythms, and deep understanding of toddler behavior. Start with the first one, with its apropos rhyming of *drama*, *mama*, and *pajama*.

### Kitten's First Full Moon
**Kevin Henkes**
This nighttime story about a kitten who thinks the moon is a bowl of milk makes toddlers laugh and feel wise and grown-up. Henkes's style in this and his many other award-winning books is very appealing—somehow gentle and lively at the same time.

### More More More, Said the Baby
**Vera B. Williams**
This exuberant modern classic features diverse babies and their families having fun throughout the day. Williams uses strategic repetition of words toddlers love, accompanied by warm, colorful art showing them tumbling around.

### I Like It When
**Mary Murphy**
With simple, graphic illustrations of a penguin parent and child sharing the activities of a typical day, this book affirms the pleasure toddlers take in

doing stuff together ("I like it when you hold my hand. I like it when you let me help"), culminating in "I love you"s that may turn you to mush.

## Peekaboo Morning
Rachel Isadora

Peekaboo fun is in full effect with this book, a sweet list of all the things your toddler is happy to wake up to see, along with delightful illustrations by the Caldecott Honor-winning artist Isadora of a brown-skinned baby—still a rarity in board books.

## Pat the Bunny AND The Telephone Book
Dorothy Kunhardt

*Pat the Bunny* is a must-have for getting your toddler involved in reading time, but try *The Telephone Book*, too. With its almost mesmerizing quality, there's a reason it has endured, despite a dated look and frankly bizarre story.

## Cook in a Book: Pancakes!
Lotta Nieminen

A genius idea: Your child "makes" pancakes by following the recipe with moving parts that let him add ingredients, "mix" the batter, and so on. If this one's a hit, try the *Tacos!* and *Pizza!* books in this series, too.

## Press Here
Hervé Tullet

So simple, so brilliant: Your child presses a dot, then another, and, as the pages turn, makes all kinds of things happen with just a swipe of a finger, sparking laughs—and a sense of creative power.

## Heads AND Tails
Matthew Van Fleet

These delightful, supremely interactive board books are heavier and bigger—and thus sturdier—than most. Your baby pulls tabs, feels textures, and moves stuff around in surprising ways as she gets to know a wide range of animals.

# CLASSICS AS BOARD BOOKS

## The Very Hungry Caterpillar
Eric Carle

This is a prime example of when to gravitate to the board-book version of a book, which won't wear, tear, and altogether deteriorate from the inevitable poking of fingers into playful cutout holes. Colorful, delicious, delightful.

## Maisy's Bedtime
Lucy Cousins

With their bright colors; strong, unique shapes; friendly, non-gender-stereotyped animal characters; and just the right amount of action and surprise, the Maisy books are ideal board books. Nearly every child goes through a Maisy phase; this simple bedtime account makes clear why.

## The Snowy Day
Ezra Jack Keats

A classic for the ages and the first mainstream picture book to center on an African American child, this story will enter your dreamscape with its beautiful vision of a perfect snowfall.

### Chicka Chicka Boom Boom
**Bill Martin Jr. and John Archambault,
illustrated by Lois Ehlert**
This hypnotic alphabet book is flat-out
fun to read, and babies want to hear
it. The simple cutout art works well as
a board book, and the amount of text
on the page is just right. Warning: The
rhyming cadences of this book may
get stuck in your head well into the
child's adolescence (but they are good
cadences, at least).

### Brown Bear, Brown Bear, What Do You See?
**Bill Martin Jr.,
illustrated by Eric Carle**
This book, and its companions (*Polar Bear,
Polar Bear, What Do You Hear?*, etc.) have
remained constants for at least three
reasons: the charming beat of the text,
the questions that beg for a call-and-
response from young children, and the
sweet collage art. This is often the first
type of book a child "reads," that is,
memorizes the words that go with the
pictures.

### The Runaway Bunny
**Margaret Wise Brown,
illustrated by Clement Hurd**
This book polarizes grown-ups, so take
a look for yourself and decide if you
want to add it to your mix. Some see
the mother bunny's devotion to her
offspring as relentless overparenting.
Others embrace it as maternal
adoration, one that captures that rush
of love. Either way: bunnies!

### Chicken Soup with Rice
**Maurice Sendak**
You can read it, you can sing it. This
Sendak classic consists of a poem about
every month, each ending hilariously in
the words *chicken soup with rice*. There's
the repetition that helps kids develop
language, along with the humor that
makes them love their favorite books.
The other three Nutshell Library books
Sendak wrote to go along with this one
are pretty great, too; all come as board
books or in their original tiny-scaled,
clothbound form.

### The Little Engine That Could
**Watty Piper**
This one's best as a board book: The
text runs continuously over the pages,
leading to lots of page turning that
otherwise could mean tearing. It's every
parent's wish that their children will
read it and likewise never give up.

### Little Blue and Little Yellow
**Leo Lionni**
This timeless story about friendship's
risks and rewards is told through
Lionni's trademark graphic art, with the
simplest circle shapes for characters. It
also operates on a profound level in its
depiction of identity and relationships.

### Bus Stops
**Taro Gomi**
The books of this prolific Japanese
author-illustrator scale down extremely
well to board books. *Bus Stops* has
appealing repetition, a surprise on every
page, and a few adventurous words set
in context.

# READING WITH TODDLERS

Gradually, and then suddenly—that's how Ernest Hemingway described going broke. More recently John Green described falling in love in a similar way: slowly, then all at once. This concept also usefully captures how a baby turns into a toddler. You see it coming, yet before you know it, it's upon you. Your once tiny, docile babe is now a force to be reckoned with, in possession of a distinct personality, able to communicate all too clearly his own needs, desires, and preferences. And he moves—sometimes very quickly. Your home becomes a riot of activity, your days a bit trickier to plan and control.

That's why it's good to have the routines and patterns of reading well in place by the time toddlerhood is fully in effect, with all its rollicking and clattering. Because as valuable as reading is to a baby, for a toddler the benefits start to skyrocket. In fact, it's hard to overestimate the greatness of reading for a toddler's intellectual, emotional, and social development. For the parents of toddlers, too, it is a godsend: If nothing else, it offers a moment of quiet in what can seem like frantic days.

Just as babies and young children benefit from hearing many different words, they also need to be exposed to a variety of information—and never more so than when they are toddlers, venturing out into the great big world for the first time. When you read with toddlers, they are really taking it in: vocabulary and language structure, numbers and math concepts, colors, shapes, flora and fauna, manners and rules of behavior, and all kinds of other useful facts about how the world works. Toddlers are constantly gathering knowledge, and there is no more efficient way to deliver it to them than through the pages of books. They go beyond just learning what the words are, to learning how to apply those words to the world around them.

That knowledge helps them navigate their lives right now—learning how to say "please," figuring out the difference between a tractor and a dump truck, understanding what makes a family—and it will be essential to their later progress as readers.

Toddlerhood is when you can use books to expand your child's world, so be sure to read them all kinds of books. Don't be afraid to expose even the smallest toddlers to subjects for which they don't have any context. All topics—from geology to the history of art to life in different cultures—can be broken down into small parts and made interesting and understandable by a great children's book. A child doesn't have to have been to a beach to read about one.

## Here's What You Need to Know

### Open Up Their Worlds

Toddlers' minds are flexible, expansive, and generous. They don't care if the main character is a boy or a girl or a hamster. Take advantage of this time to expose them to a balanced cast in their books, and help children of both sexes spend time with themes that might seem exclusively or stereotypically "boy oriented" (say, trucks, machinery, sports) or "girl oriented" (say, friendship, cooking, fairies). Seek out books that show girls being active and assertive and boys being sensitive and nurturing. Books that feature a protagonist whose gender is not clear are great, too (animals! robots!), for implanting the idea that gender roles and identities don't have to be set in stone, and that beyond "masculine" or "feminine" is simply "human."

### Reflect the Real World

What holds true for gender also holds true for race, culture, class, and geographic borders. It's getting easier to find books with racially and ethnically diverse characters in them, at long last. Make a point of reading these to your child. If your child is a member of a racial or ethnic minority, it's

especially important to seek out books that feature children who look similar to yours. All children need to see themselves reflected in stories. But no matter what your child's background happens to be, find books that casually show people with different skin tones and ethnicities building a rocket ship or exploring an underwater cavern or simply going to the grocery store with Grandpa. Bring them stories that present the variety of cultural traditions and family structures and life experiences that coexist in our communities. As you read with them, you're helping prepare them for life in a diverse world—and you're helping to build their capacity for empathy. (See our lists in Part Five of books that are especially strong on building empathy and kindness, pages 171 to 176.) Books are a great way to "try on" other people's experiences, and toddlers are at a developmental point where they need to start understanding how other people feel—and treating them accordingly.

Literacy experts talk about the need for a child to be exposed to books that are both "mirrors and windows"—some should be mirrors in which a child can see herself reflected, and others should be windows into the experiences of people who are different. By giving your toddler both kinds of books, you're helping with the task of learning how to value and respect himself while also valuing and respecting others.

## Develop Rituals Around Reading

As toddlerhood settles in and preschool is upon you, there are still, of course, the emotional benefits of regular reading that began when your child was a baby. Each time you read to him, your toddler is experiencing the connection between books and the familiar, beloved sound of your voice—that physical closeness reading together brings. You're continuing to build a deeply positive association with books that will last a lifetime.

But even if you're totally on board with the idea, there is still the matter of working reading into your busy days. Bedtime reading is a familiar nightly routine for parents of toddlers, and it's probably the easiest way to guarantee some reading every day. There may be no sweeter part of parenthood than the ritual of reading books before your child falls asleep. Make sure there's time for a picture book (or three, or four . . .). Keep the atmosphere around bedtime soothing and not rushed, and choose some of the many books that end, strategically, with a peaceful going-to-bed scene (though friskier books about sleep-avoiding children are fun, too). It's a great way to get your little ball of energy to unwind before bed, and it's a good habit to nurture now so that nightly reading time is completely ingrained in both of you by the elementary school years.

But try to read with your toddler during the day as well. Be open to grabbing a spontaneous five minutes with a book or two here and there, even during weekday mornings. Read while waiting for the bus or car pool. Read while they linger over breakfast. Offering to read with toddlers is one of the best ways—some days, it can seem like the only way—to get them to slow down and focus. For you as well as your kid, it's a treat to be able to sit close and enjoy these moments of connection while it's still light outside.

Daytime reading is easier if you make sure books are a significant physical presence in your home and you remember to bring a few with you when you're out and about. Stick two or three in your stroller or diaper bag for your child to look at in the car, on the bus, in a café, in a doctor's office. Rather than passing your child a cell phone or toy while you're standing in a long line, you can give him a familiar book that he loves and knows by heart, or squat down and read a new story to him.

Whereas with very young babies, the choice of what to read is all yours, now is the time when you can get a handle on your child's preferences. Your child is probably already surprising you with independent tastes and opinions. Just as she doesn't like your kale salad, she may not appreciate the exquisite black-and-white pen-and-ink artistry of Robert McCloskey's *Make Way for Ducklings* as much as you may have as a child. At the same time, you may not be all that excited about fairies or talking trucks, but your child might be. Support that. Encourage children to express what *they* like about their books, and find more books like those.

## Pro Tips for Reading Out Loud

Reading to a child should be a pas de deux, not a solo performance. The more you can make reading mutually satisfying, the more it will be associated with pleasure and reward. Early childhood experts like to say that we read a book out loud *with* a child, rather than *to* a child. There's a huge difference.

• Find the most comfortable reading position for the two of you. Laps are always a good starting point, since they give you a maximum physical connection, but sometimes toddlers prefer side-by-side. For a change of pace, try sitting face-to-face with your child and showing the books to her. Some toddlers may even scoot away, to listen from a spot across the room, and that's okay, too. The point is to experiment until you find your happy place—or places.

• Always begin with the title of the book and the name of the author and illustrator. This will teach an appreciation for the creation of books and allow the child to begin to identify favorite authors and pick up on similar artistic styles. Spend some time looking at the cover and talking about it. If it's

appropriate, ask, "What do you think this one is going to be about?"

• Don't just read the book—read the room! If your child doesn't like your silly ogre's voice, don't use it. Alas, this isn't about you. Sometimes, our own zany characterizations charm us more than they do our listeners. (We have both learned this the hard way. It's a bummer when your child doesn't appreciate your thespian eccentricities.)

• If something you're reading isn't working for you or your child, change it. You can summarize a passage that seems too long to hold the attention of your little audience. You can substitute an easier word for a word you know is beyond your child's comprehension. You can soften the harsh words that come out of the mouths of fictional parents and adults from earlier eras, who scolded the young folk in a critical, relentless way that can shock and puzzle today's kids. The little old woman in the shoe doesn't *have* to beat her children, after all. And as we mentioned earlier, you can "clean up" a book that is racially insensitive or sexist.

• Interruptions show that your child is engaged. Don't get so caught up in your own reading that you ignore your child's comments and queries. If you find yourself saying, "Just let me finish this page," stop and ask your child to repeat the question.

• Let her turn the pages and take charge of the pace. (It's also great for developing fine-motor skills.) Having this measure of control makes them feel like part of the process.

• Read a bit more slowly than you might think is natural, and savor the rhythm of the text. Draw out the especially interesting or funny moments. Board books and picture books are akin to poetry in their awareness of the sounds of words and their arrangement on the page. Many picture book authors use the turn of a page to create delicious suspense. Try singing some books—or some passages—if the mood strikes. Many bedtime books feel like they're almost meant to be sung rather than read. Your child will grow up remembering these made-for-her tunes.

• Keep in mind that your child isn't always reading quite the same story you are. As you're reading out loud, with your mind focused on the text, and the child is listening to your words, she is, at the same time, following the story through the illustrations. She might see things you don't see. She may laugh at something that's only in the pictures, or notice goblins lurking unmentioned in the corner of a spread. If your child doesn't seem engaged by the words, ask what she sees in the pictures. Sometimes there's a second story in there. Often children glean information visually that is not explicitly stated in the written narrative. Have them explain it to you.

• With toddlers, point at objects on the page and invite them to tell you what they are. Casually offer more information if you can. With preschoolers, invite them to tell you what is going on in the pictures.

## It's Okay to Hate Some Children's Books

You are human: You have limits. Let's say there's a certain book that drives you nuts but that your 3-year-old requests so often, you find yourself toying with the idea of sneaking it into the compost. Don't despair! You can occasionally pry a child loose from certain vexing favorites. When Pamela's eldest went through a Biscuit phase, she and her husband quickly wearied of *woof-woofing* aloud. After a certain period of indulgence, the

Biscuit books became mysteriously harder to locate on the shelves, where other books about pets and animal antics somehow materialized in their place. Don't deny toddlers the books they like, but it's okay sometimes to steer them toward other, similar books. (Once that daughter was older, she loved hearing the tale of the "lost" Biscuits.)

### The Benefits of Memory

Some books you will find you can quickly memorize. Or memorize after having read them aloud fifteen times. If a certain ennui has settled into your reading routine, do not despair. You can vary the way you read a book—or you can simply tune out and "read" it by rote while letting your mind wander where it will. Don't feel too guilty: Captivated young listeners often won't notice; they're too caught up in their own enjoyment. Moreover, they may have memorized the book themselves.

### Is She Reading?!

Around this time, a glorious moment may arrive. You may find your toddler turning the pages of a board book, absorbed, all on her own. She may be reciting words she knows by heart. She may be looking at the pictures. Take a moment to recognize that *she is becoming a reader*. The part where she makes out individual words and sentences will come in due time, but meanwhile, what she's doing right now—following a narrative, getting information visually, becoming riveted by what she sees on pages—is all part of the big picture of reading. Call it that. You can say to her, "Oh, wow! Did you realize you're *reading* this book?" She will begin to see herself as a reader, too. Say it with pride and pleasure, but also say it as though it is merely a basic, incontrovertible fact about her. Because, thanks to you, it is.

In this way, you can take part in building your child's identity as a reader. A positive attitude toward reading goes only so far—your child also has to think of reading as something she *does*, an activity she chooses so often and so reflexively, it helps define her.

That means reading should be a strong part of his very identity, from toddlerhood on into preschool and kindergarten—well before he can "officially" read, in other words. Are you packing for a trip? Just as automatically as you ask your son to choose pajamas or remind him not to forget his stuffed rabbit, ask, "What books are you bringing?" Has he come back from a playdate at a friend's house? Ask, "What books does Sean like to read? Does he like *Dragons Love Tacos*, too?" When someone asks what your child enjoys doing, say, "He loves to read."

## Libraries Are Great For . . .

• *Storytelling hours:* Many libraries have special rooms or areas in their children's library for storytelling, often with pillows and stuffed animals strewn around. It's a great place to meet up with other parent-friends while your kids are well occupied and also a good place for them to be with children their age.

• *Author visits:* Libraries love to host local or visiting authors, and what a special way for your children to learn about the real people behind the books. They'll start understanding that books are created by people like them.

• *Community events for the whole family:* Libraries will host lectures by local historians or experts, movie nights— often films based on

books—book clubs, chess clubs, slide shows, and other great occasions for breaking the usual household or neighborhood routine.

• *Free computer access with kid-friendly games:* If you don't want your kids to have regular access to a computer at home or your personal computer is strictly for work, consider making the library their computer time and place. Computers set up in the children's library are often loaded with librarian-vetted programs geared specifically to young people.

• *A quiet place to read:* Sometimes you just have to get out of the house—even if it's just to sack out in someone else's armchair. Your children, too, will appreciate the change in scenery.

### The Family Library

The term alone sounds rather grand, suggesting a beautifully appointed room filled with floor-to-ceiling bookshelves with a rolling ladder, handsome volumes shelved alphabetically according to genre, subject, provenance. But that's not necessarily what we're envisioning here. What a family library really means is a collection of books shared among family members. Those books might be stuffed into a nook in the kitchen or piled on the floor of the living room or scattered throughout the house wherever there is empty shelf space. In fact, although it is lovely to have a special place for books, there's also an advantage to having books a little bit everywhere, woven into the very fabric of home life, whether it's a book perched on the toilet tank in a bathroom or an elegant stack on a coffee table in the living room.

According to studies that measure the likelihood of a child growing up to be a reader, the most important factor is not how well reading was taught in the child's school, nor the number of hours spent reading aloud to the child. Regardless of the parents' income level or education, the statistic most highly correlated to literacy is the number of books present in the home.

In a way, it's obvious. Children become readers when they have ample occasion to read. We know that kids who want to read will track down those opportunities—whether it's on a road sign or on the back of a cereal box. But if you want to increase the likelihood that your child will read, you should fill your house with books. Fill it with temptation.

Filling up a house with books is a joy and a pleasure, and an ongoing treasure hunt. It's an impulse for many and an obsession for not a few of us (guilty!). And it need not break your budget. Brand-new books can be quite pricey, but used books can be almost criminally cheap. Great used and discounted books can be found at library sales, bookstore sales, school sales, in used bookstores, and through online sellers. Books are available literally for pennies, and the cost often has little to do with the quality of the physical book itself. Do not worry about building your collection with perfect volumes; books are meant to be *read*, and well-worn books are like living artifacts, their curled or worn or even marked-up pages the record of many happy readers. A hand-me-down book, even one inscribed from one stranger to another, can feel like an heirloom, a precious piece of history. One of the greatest pop-up phenomena that have sprouted in many communities are Little Free Libraries—book kiosks where people drop off books they're finished with and pick up new ones their neighbors have left. What a great way to show kids that reading books opens them up to a community of readers.

## The Modern Library

Make regular trips to the library—even better as a family—to keep a constant stream of new and intriguing books around the house. Many local libraries have no limits on the number you can take out at one time. And keeping a constantly rotating menu on hand exposes children to a variety of subjects, formats, and genres, piquing their curiosity. If your kids are online, show them the website of the local library, where they can browse the collection and reserve books that they can then pick up for themselves when they're available. How delightful for a child to find an email addressed to him, notifying him that his book has arrived from an interlibrary loan system.

## Think Outside the Book Box

Even the smallest children can occasionally meander beyond strictly-for-children books. So-called coffee table books are a prime example. Although it may not occur to you that your child would want to look through a monograph of Matisse or the latest work by an avant-garde photographer, she may surprise you. Children love visuals, and their worlds will be vastly expanded if there are tempting books of eye-catching nature photography, artwork, comics, landscapes, and travel scenes scattered on tabletops in rooms where they might throw themselves on the sofa one bored afternoon. So be aware of all the ways you can create impromptu reading opportunities for your child. Discovered on a living room table, a big, visual, information-rich book like David Macaulay's *The Way Things Work* can be an ongoing temptation for children of all ages. But don't stop there. Leave paperbacks and magazines piled in the bathroom (yes, everyone reads on the toilet, even kids) or anywhere they could catch a young reader's eye. Speaking of toilets, here's a bonus tip: For toddlers who can make their way through board books or wordless books on their own, or are in an eager stage of beginning to identify words, reading while on the toilet can be a boon for potty training.

### A Bookshelf of One's Own

If room permits—and there's almost always a way—let your child build a personal collection and keep it in his room. If possible, get him his own bookcase or small standing bookshelf. If you have the space when your children are still toddlers, look for the kind of bookshelf that allows you to place books face out (they're popular at tag sales). But don't get too caught up in the display—after all, the point of books on a shelf is for them to come *off* the shelf. From babyhood on, keep a bunch of books easily accessible—especially active, lift-the-flap ones or fun oversized ones—whenever you're putting together a playtime setup, whether on a floor, rug, or play mat.

### Children Love Collecting

Whether it's Beanie Babies or, later, Hot Wheels cars or baseball cards, kids are natural gatherers. Make your child's book collection a point of personal pride and identity. The books your child gloms on to—whether by subject, theme, or illustrator—reflect who he is at any given moment. Your child will cycle through these books, wanting to discard old favorites for new books—but don't be so quick to throw them out. If you have limited shelf space in your kid's bedroom, move books in and out, storing away ones that have fallen out of favor. Pull them out again in several months or a year and see if she is delighted to rediscover books she loved "long ago."

## Saving for Posterity

If possible, hold on to a few of your kids' most loved books. This may not be practical for the well-loved books of toddlerhood, but start keeping the idea in mind now. Children's books are a lifelong treasure for many people. Clothbound copies of Louisa May Alcott, as well as a first edition of *A Light in the Attic*, are still part of Pamela's collection and have taken turns on her kids' shelves. The same goes for Maria's copies of *Sylvester and the Magic Pebble* and *James and the Giant Peach*. One of the great things about returning to your childhood home as an adult is rediscovering the books in your old bedroom, if your parents held on to them. Think about how precious those rediscoveries are. Do the same for your kids.

## Kid Librarian

Show children from the earliest age that books are not only for receiving and reading; they are also for giving. Some books you'll be glad to get rid of, some books they'll be ready to give up, and some books, they will learn, will be especially appreciated by a friend, younger cousin, or teacher. Show them also how great it is to donate books in good condition to shelters, doctors' offices, schools, fund-raising sales, or local libraries.

## "Goody Bag" Books

Most parents have some aspect of modern parenting culture they just can't get into a groove with, and for us it's the unrelenting hoo-ha of birthday-party excess. At a certain point, each of us found that the more we could integrate books into our children's and their friends' birthdays, the better we felt.

To start with, there's nothing better than a book for a birthday party gift. Not only is it more rewarding to think of your child's friend owning a copy of Emily Jenkins's *Toys Go Out* rather than another plastic horse with fake hair, but it can become a nice excuse to make regular trips to your neighborhood indie bookstore—a place that no doubt also does a beautiful job wrapping.

If you're the one throwing the party, we invite you to say goodbye, forever, to the wasteful and cavity-inducing practice of handing out goody bags at the end: Have a birthday-party book swap instead. Ask guests to wrap one of their own used books in good condition and bring it to the party. On the way out, everyone gets to choose a wrapped book. Don't forget to also wrap one from the birthday child—and let her pick first. It's far nicer for both child and parent than going home with candy or cheap plastic toys and clearly demonstrates to children that books are something special; they mark an occasion, and provide a happy ending. With older children, you might have guests bring an unwrapped book and let them choose from the pile. Determine the order by pulling numbers from a hat or through a contest or game. Or if you're not sure how a swap will go over, just give out gently used books from your child's collection in lieu of goody bags. We promise you—other parents won't think you're cheap; they'll be *grateful*.

**The Book of the Year**

Another birthday book idea: Give your child one special book for every birthday in his life, to be kept in a special place on his shelf. Inscribe it to him on the occasion of his second, third, fourth birthday—there's no reason to ever stop this tradition. In that inscription, tell him why you decided to get him that particular book that year. Perhaps it was a book you loved when you were 4. Or a book your grandmother gave to you when you were that age. Maybe the book's hero is also a 4-year-old from Minneapolis or a boy who loves baseball. Include a line or two about what he's like at this age. Yes, of course, he knows that stuff now. But think what it will be like for him to pick up that birthday book when he's 7 and read about what he was like at 4. It's amazing how young the sense of nostalgia starts. (Wait until your child gets old enough to ask to see her baby book. Again, and again.) Every year, seeing that little library of birthday books will be a gift all its own.

### Dedicated

If a book hasn't been dedicated by the giver, ask your toddler what he remembers about getting the book and who gave it to him. Inscribe the first page with these thoughts, in his words. It's these kinds of personalized touches that make a child's first library so special.

### Bookstores Love Babies

There are periods in your life when you spend a lot of time in libraries, and there are other periods when getting to the library is not as practical. For many new parents, going to a bookstore regularly is actually a more appealing and workable option. Or at least a fun alternative. For one thing: *coffee*. If you are caring for a newborn or chasing a toddler for hours a day, need we say more? Most bookstores now either have their own café or are conveniently located on a block with a good café nearby.

Independent bookstores, especially, have been making themselves ever more attractive to new parents in recent years. Take advantage! The staff tends to be passionate and knowledgeable, and there is usually at least one person who really knows children's books. There is always a children's section with an environment designed to welcome your child for a blessed half hour or so: comfy chairs, mats, and perhaps even toys or blocks or a train table she can play with alongside all the books. Many bookstores are even specifically focused on children's books. If you're living near one of those, count yourself lucky, and ask for recommendations.

Bookstores tend to have even more author appearances than libraries, and often they have free read-aloud story times and book clubs for kids or teenagers. If your budget is tight, buying your child a book can feel even more justifiable when you are supporting a local business that adds so much to the community—and gives you a friendly place to stop by, browse, and relax for a bit when you and your child are out and about. Bookstore sales clerks are often just as passionate about the books they surround themselves with as librarians are, and eager to share their own suggestions and offer if-you-like-this-you-may-like-that advice.

# What to Look For: Toddler Books

### Start with Picture Books

Picture books are bigger than board books, with regular (rippable) pages and, usually, a slightly longer, more developed story. You may have introduced picture books back in the newborn days, but the sweet spot is later toddlerhood and beyond. Your child's awareness of the world is always expanding, and picture books will engage that part of him. They help him understand and navigate the stages of life and all the vicissitudes of growing up: a new sibling, the beginning of school, conflict with a friend, fear of the dark, picky eating, and on and on. They bring the world out there to life, help her make sense of it, and open up new worlds.

### Sweet Harmony

Look for the connection between excellent illustration and transcendent words. As with board books, the images aren't there merely to accompany the words—they work in tandem with text to tell the story. This means that often, a crucial piece of information is delivered not in words, but in a picture.

### The Author-Illustrator in One

Some of the all-time great picture books are by an author who also illus trates (or an illustrator who also writes, depending on your point of view). You probably know them—Maurice Sendak, Dr. Seuss, Leo Lionni, Jerry Pinkney, Lois Ehlert, Taro Gomi. There are many masters of the form, able to combine their written voice with their artistic talent to create a whole, distinct world.

### The Author-Illustrator Pairing

Books created by an author-illustrator team can be just as delightful. Often the author is regularly paired with the same illustrator for most books—or for a series of books with the same character, such as recent collaborations between the writer Mac Barnett and the illustrator Jon Klassen.

### Attention to the Details

Every inch of a picture book is thought out, from the cover to the "end-papers," those pages attached to the covers that aren't part of the narrative. Feel free to judge these books by their covers—and look underneath the jackets as well, because often you'll find a surprise hidden on the reverse side and on the cover of the book itself: an entirely different cover, often with a joke or some extra information. Picture book publishers have become incredibly ambitious and creative in thinking about the entire package. The endpapers are often marvels of patterning and graphic design. The title pages of picture books are often full-fledged illustrations that offer a kind of preamble to the story within.

### Books That Don't Get Old

The all-time great picture books tend to stay delightful to adults even with frequent repetition. *Harold and the Purple Crayon*, *The Lorax*, and *The Story About Ping* are books you can read out loud repeatedly and not lose your sanity. Once your child asks for a book that does get old, you'll know it—and will appreciate these phenomenal books all the more.

### Books That Let You Look Beyond Words

Don't fall into the trap of thinking the more text in the book, the more value you get. Although it's easy to think this way, especially since picture books can be pricey, the quality of the book really doesn't increase with the quantity of the text or the number of pages. Some of the all-time greatest picture books are wordless, like Jerry Pinkney's *The Lion & the Mouse*, David Wiesner's *Flotsam*, and Suzy Lee's *Wave*. Wordless books are a fantastic opportunity to build your child's visual literacy and help teach him how to decipher images to understand a story or get information. Invite your child to tell you what is happening on each page and then ask, "What makes you say that?" You can also endlessly reinvent the story, adapting it, enriching it, and tailoring it to your child's mood, day, and age. In David Wiesner's wordless book *Mr. Wuffles!*, a group of aliens enter the world of a somewhat grumpy cat. Their language is expressed in pure symbols; it's up to you and your child to decide what it sounds like when "read."

## Books That Use Animals

The ranks of great picture books have always been heavy with animal protagonists like Little Bear, Frog and Toad, and Pete the Cat. It's not just that children love animals—the critters in their books help them reflect on problems from a safe emotional distance. Sometimes it's easier admitting to fear or anxiety if you're relating to a distraught sea otter. Animals are also often gender neutral and appeal to both sexes. And although stories about animals can be a good way to talk about racism, race is a solely human concept, of course—animals themselves have no race. They are universal.

## Books That Make Facts Fun

Not every picture book has to tell a story. Many of the most memorable ones approach their role differently: They show fascinating information about life, often broken up into bite-sized chunks. Many nonfiction picture books use outstanding art to help tell narrative historical stories or explain scientific topics. For some children, picture books that are organized like catalogs or encyclopedias are even more compelling than fictional stories, and even the most story-loving child likes to occasionally get lost in these "fact books." These are also books kids can "read" by themselves. The books of Richard Scarry, with his busy, multifaceted, and densely populated landscapes of raccoons and pigs and an improbably charismatic worm, for example, give children a lot of stuff to look at and sneak in mini-stories that don't require a long commitment. Many people (including us) have vivid memories of reading *Richard Scarry's Busy, Busy World* at an age well before we actually knew how to read.

### Books That Teach—Without Being Obvious About It

Great picture books reinforce the act of learning to read, but in a subtle, fun, and unforced way. A picture book can directly address the letters of the alphabet (*Take Away the A* by Michaël Escoffier, illustrated by Kris Di Giacomo, and *Z Is for Moose* by Kelly Bingham, illustrated by Paul Zelinsky) or use vocabulary- and grammar-building wordplay (*I Yam a Donkey!* by Cece Bell, and *You're Pulling My Leg!* by Pat Street and Eric Brace). They can even support your child's growing numeracy (*Two Mice* by Sergio Ruzzier, *A Chair for My Mother* by Vera B. Williams, and *Goodnight Numbers* by Danica McKellar). Children will hardly notice these aspects of good picture books. But they will learn. And they'll like it.

### Books That Are Recognized

A picture book that has certain medals on its cover is always worth a look. In the United States, the awards given annually by the American Library Association (ALA) are the gold standard. The ALA's Caldecott Medal and Caldecott Honors are given for the best overall picture books. Likewise the ALA's Coretta Scott King, Pura Belpré, and Robert F. Sibert awards honor the best African American, Latino, and nonfiction books of the year.

## Be Wary Of

### Bogus Medals

When you see those shiny stickers on a picture book's cover indicating an award it has won, do read the fine print. Some "awards" are simply marketing schemes or paid industry endorsements that have not been vetted by outside experts. You can always ask a librarian or experienced children's bookseller if you're wondering about an award.

### Didacticism

It is true that books teach children many things. But most children's problems cannot be "fixed" in one book, especially if they are banged over the head with the lesson, to the detriment of story basics like character, emotion, and plot. If you're looking for a book to guide a child through tough challenges like learning how to initiate a friendship, how to abstain from annoying behaviors, how to handle bullying or overcome shyness, those books are out there. But choose carefully. Humor is often the spoonful of sugar these kinds of books need. And here is one more caveat: Some kids absolutely adore didactic moral tales and instructional stories. The key is to know your child, because the last thing you want is for him to sit squirming through stories that embarrass or annoy him or make him feel bad about himself.

### Who Is This For?!

Picture books can be written for children, and picture books can be written for children and for grown-ups. But children's picture books should not be written for grown-ups alone. The perfect balance is the Pixar formula: getting kids to giggle over *Toy Story 3* or *Inside Out* while their grown-up companions are overcome with emotion, nostalgia, and tears right beside them. Get it wrong and you've got potty humor combined with grown-up pop-culture asides. Believe it or not, this can happen in picture books, too, though usually the off-key notes are of a gentler nature. Consider whether the book looks at the world in a way a child might. The picture book that seems geared to adults, with kids only casually in mind, tends to be visually stunning but otherwise utterly lacking in the things that engage children, such as humor, silliness, and brightness. These books look like they belong in a museum store, and often they are sold there. They leave most kids bored silly. The same goes for those wink-wink parody books that really are just for the grown-ups.

### When the Moral Is the Story

Another "least favorite" category: drony morality tales like the ones in The Berenstain Bears series, in which a bunch of animals or kids or aliens misbehave for twenty-eight pages, only to be berated and set onto the correct path in the final four pages. Critics have pointed out that these books take so much time describing the bad behavior that they unintentionally provide a model of bullying and brattiness rather than instilling the often unbelievable and unrealistic lesson at the end. Books can do a far better job of proving a behavioral point with nuanced characters and, best of all, humor. For example, *I'm Bored* by Michael Ian Black, illustrated by Debbie Ridpath Ohi, in which a potato—you have to trust us here—constantly complains to an idle child that it's bored, at one point muttering, "Snoring!" It is far more effective than, say, a story in which a parent berates two children for lying around the house all day doing nothing.

## Books Starring TV Characters

Sometimes, publishers take advantage of TV shows' popularity by churning out books based on franchised TV characters with minimal investment in literary and artistic value. Books about TV characters are often made by ever-changing teams of authors and illustrators, causing inconsistency and market glut. And books based on TV characters can make kids crave even more TV time. If your kid absolutely demands a book starring Peppa Pig, there's no great harm done by indulging her—it *is* a book, after all—but try to keep these in check.

# Our Picture Book Picks

## TRUE CLASSICS

### The Amazing Bone
**William Steig**
Can a pig named Pearl and her new friend, a small talking bone, outwit a band of robbers *and* a hungry fox? Like every Steig book, the just slightly fantastical story sucks you in so completely, the pages turn themselves. You will want to hug this book. And while we're on Steig: *Gorky Rises, Brave Irene, Caleb and Kate,* and *Sylvester and the Magic Pebble* are all gems. Steig is a master.

### The Carrot Seed
**Ruth Krauss,**
**illustrated by Crockett Johnson**
This book teaches the patience and technique needed to plant a seed and help it grow, with a satisfying "I told you so!" ending.

### Millions of Cats
**Wanda Gág**
An old man and an old woman decide to get a cat, and end up with not one, but millions and billions and trillions of cats. Published in the 1920s—proof that absurdist preschool humor is timeless.

### Harold and the Purple Crayon
**Crockett Johnson**
Armed only with an oversized purple crayon, young Harold draws himself a landscape full of wonder and excitement. This is perhaps *the* classic story about the power of imagination.

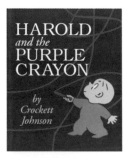

### The Little House
**Virginia Lee Burton**
An old-fashioned farmhouse faces encroaching development. The house, drawn sweetly to resemble a face, with curtains as eyelids on its window eyes, tugs at your heart. Don't worry: There's a happy ending.

### A Tree Is Nice
**Janice May Udry,**
**illustrated by Marc Simont**
Simple and incantational, this ode to all that trees bring into our lives is a great example of a picture book that doesn't tell a story but merely arranges the facts of a child's world into something profound and beautiful.

### Frederick
**Leo Lionni**
Another story your child may cherish for a lifetime: Frederick is a mouse who seems idle while others gather food for winter, but when the food runs out, it turns out Frederick has been collecting words to make poems that comfort and inspire everyone.

### The House on East 88th Street
**Bernard Waber**
The first book about Lyle the Crocodile and his human New York City family features dramatic storytelling, timeless humor, and a surprisingly tender heart.

### Caps for Sale
**Esphyr Slobodkina**
With its groovy visuals and monkey-see, monkey-do plot, this tale of a man selling caps that are swiped by some mischievous monkeys has been delighting children for generations.

### Moon Man
**Tomi Ungerer**
It's hard to pick a favorite Tomi Ungerer, but this one is especially easy to love: The Moon comes down to Earth to join the festivities he sees, and dances blissfully at a garden party before he's thrown into jail by people afraid of his differentness. Luckily, he escapes and is rocketed back home by a friendly scientist.

## NEW CLASSICS

### Don't Let the Pigeon Drive the Bus!
**Mo Willems**
Willems's wiseacre Pigeon—a streetwise and snappy little bird who just wants to drive the bus—has become a childhood icon, and his books are great for getting

kids actively involved in story time. Start with this one, then read them all.

### The Stray Dog
**Marc Simont**
A stray finds a new home in this emotionally astute, gorgeously illustrated tale of kids getting parents to change their minds, adapted from a Japanese tale. If there's no way your family is getting a dog, be careful with this one.

### Everywhere Babies
**Susan Meyers,**
**illustrated by Marla Frazee**
It is very possible that nobody draws a cuter and more expressive baby than Marla Frazee. These babies do every single cute thing babies do, to the rapt delight of every child and grown-up around them.

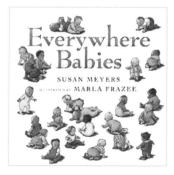

### Train, Farm, AND Beach
**Elisha Cooper**
For kids who are curious about the everyday world—that is, all kids—these gorgeous nonfiction books are endlessly absorbing, with the meticulousness and aesthetic interest of Old Master paintings.

### Flotsam
**David Wiesner**
Wiesner is a master of the wordless book. This one starts with a kid who finds a camera on a beach, and builds into a time-traveling puzzle. The art looks realistic, until it tips over the surrealist edge.

### Hello Lighthouse
**Sophie Blackall**
A knockout of a book that traces the history of one lighthouse over several generations to show the danger, drama, and heroism of a way of life that's forever gone. It captures the bittersweet passing of time and the eternal beauty of the sea.

### Shadow
**Suzy Lee**
A little girl with a flashlight creates a magical world of shadows in this playful yet sophisticated, nearly wordless book by a remarkable talent—check out Lee's *Wave* and *Lines*, too.

### Knick-Knack Paddywhack!
**Paul O. Zelinsky**
It's the old schoolyard rhyme reimagined as a boy's daydream, with lift-the-flap art that is an absolute marvel of paper engineering. It will thrill little ones and make grown-ups do double takes, too.

### Du Iz Tak?
**Carson Ellis**
An original, funny marvel of a book about the life cycle of a plant told through an invented bug language that children somehow understand. The characters are all insects, and

the fanciful, detailed art and story are splendid.

### They Say Blue
**Jillian Tamaki**

For children, the changing seasons and times of day are magical. This deeply sensory exploration of nature and the passing of time through the lens of color will captivate young eyes with its beauty.

## PICTURE BOOKS FOR BEDTIME

### In the Night Kitchen
**Maurice Sendak**

Mickey wakes in the middle of the night and ends up in a kitchen as bakers prepare morning cake. It's a great dream-adventure for kids. And pay close attention to the art: Sendak embedded lots of visual meaning for grown-ups to catch.

### Good Night, Gorilla
**Peggy Rathmann**

"Good night, Gorilla," says the zookeeper. But the mischievous gorilla isn't quite ready for bed. This nearly wordless book offers parents the opportunity to tailor the story each time, balancing familiarity with improvisation for a mixture of routine and surprise.

### 10 Minutes till Bedtime
**Peggy Rathmann**

There is much comic pleasure in this boy's bedtime routine. Even with very few words, it can be read fifteen different ways and then some.

### Time for Bed
**Mem Fox,**
**illustrated by Jane Dyer**

The mesmerizing round of good nights between farm animal parents and offspring will lull children into a cozy state of near somnolence. After this book, your work will be done.

### A Book of Sleep
**Il Sung Na**

Using a combination of painted oils, ink drawings, and digital manipulation, Na adds whimsy to his animal creatures, turning each spread into a dreamscape.

## Goodnight, Goodnight, Construction Site
**Sherri Duskey Rinker, illustrated by Tom Lichtenheld**

If your little one is a vehicle lover, the genius of this book will be completely obvious. Even skeptics will be won over by the big, warm emotions of Rinker and Lichtenheld's cooperative machinery.

## Thank You and Good Night
**Patrick McDonnell**

McDonnell's adorable and gently profound bedtime story about three animal friends having a sleepover effortlessly mixes silliness, wonder, and gratitude.

## I Am Not Sleepy and I Will Not Go to Bed
**Lauren Child**

The binge-worthy Charlie and Lola books feature one of the most adorable and winning older brother–younger sister pairs out there. This is one of their best outings: It's no surprise that Lola's bedtime requires all Charlie's reserves of ingenuity.

## The Way Home in the Night
**Akiko Miyakoshi**

In this dreamy, enchantingly illustrated book imported from Japan, with art in dusky, soft charcoal and pastels, a rabbit is carried home by her parents through city streets, noticing all the ways the world shuts down as bedtime nears.

## Owl Babies
**Martin Waddell, illustrated by Patrick Benson**

Three baby owls wake up at night worried to find their mother missing— but of course she comes back, and they all settle down to sleep in this reassuring, beautifully illustrated tale. Plus . . . baby owls!

# PART TWO

# Growing a Reader

*The two significant steps to reading take place next. We address them in two sections: "Your Emerging Reader" and "The Independent Reader."*

# YOUR EMERGING READER

All parents ask themselves the same question: When will my child begin reading? That magical breakthrough moment—when your child shows an interest in letters and begins to make out words on a page or out in the world—occurs at different ages for different children, even within the same family. Some children are 4 when it happens, others are 6 or 7. Sometimes it happens earliest with the oldest child in a family; other times, with the youngest. Pamela and Maria both had the very common experience of watching their daughters, the oldest child in both families, learn to read about a year earlier than their brothers did. The brains of girls are often ready to start reading at a younger age than the brains of boys. For both sexes, most parents describe a long period in which a child doesn't always keep letters straight or can't quite make out words, then a quick burst of comprehension, and then more regular but still sudden leaps, until one day she makes it through a short sentence. It can really seem like magic. So don't rush it.

Every child learns to read at a personal pace. There is no "correct" age for independent reading and no special formula for getting every child to read by, say, age 5½. In fact, few 5-year-olds are ready to do full-on independent reading, even though many kindergarten programs are structured toward that goal.

If you've been focused on raising a reader until now, you should feel confident your child is taking the steps toward independent reading at the pace that's personally right for him.

Wait a minute, you might say. There's a 4-year-old in your child's preschool class who is already reading chapter books. The kindergarten teacher says your son is "a little slow" in picking up phonics. Your child says he's reading, but he seems only to have memorized the text. Your older child was already reading at this point. You and your wife were both huge readers as kids; why isn't your child showing an interest in books?

These kinds of concerns plague nearly every parent of a young child, except, perhaps, the parent of that 4-year-old reader—who is surely agonizing over her child's inability to eat anything that isn't white, or his refusal to put on boots. We all have our worries. But the fact is that worries about when or how fast your kid learns to read are not well founded. The overwhelming likelihood is that whatever the pace of your child's entry into the ranks of independent readers, you have nothing to fret about. (We'll talk about some legitimate causes of concern shortly.) Just as everyone is fond of the idea that Albert Einstein was a late talker, many parents can boast that their "late" readers turned out to be voracious and sophisticated readers. Among Pamela's three children, for example, the latest to read turned out to be the most sophisticated reader and enthusiastic writer.

In fact, there is evidence that children *should* learn to read later, after their minds have developed more and after particular coding and visual scanning skills have improved. In Germany, children don't begin reading instruction until age 6 or 7. In most Scandinavian schools, children don't begin formal reading lessons until age 7. Nobody would accuse those countries of fostering illiteracy. The idea is that because many perfectly bright children are simply not able to process the steps of independent reading before age 6 or 7, it's better to focus instructional time on other kinds of learning—math, science, art, music, social skills. When children are able to master reading, they will have the knowledge base to grapple with far richer stories than those accessible to a preschooler. With this model, the very first stages of reading can be much more rewarding. Alas, this notion hasn't taken hold in most of the United States, with the exception of some progressive schools, international schools, Montessori schools, and Waldorf-affiliated schools.

# Here's What You Need to Know

### Lose the Fear of "Late"

Anything that feels "late" can cause worry in the moment, but most of us don't stew over the long-term implications of how and when our children develop each and every life skill. Do you think about the repercussions if your child mastered the playground climber a bit later than his friends or learned to tie his shoelaces at an older age? Of course not. The timing of the vast majority of childhood milestones—including reading—does not correlate with later cognitive or physical function or skills. And yet many kids are forced or pushed or even somewhat prodded to learn to read earlier than they are ready, which can lead to a lot of unnecessary frustration as they stare at a page without anything clicking in their brains. Why not step back and look to your child for signs that the time is right?

### Accentuate the Positive

Regardless of your child's age and stage of reading, always keep your emotional responses to reading positive. Share your excitement about books with your child while maintaining a studious lack of concern, and maybe even a little bit of fuzziness, over exactly where he is in the learning-to-read scheme. Encourage other caregivers in your child's circle to do the same; a grandmother or babysitter who constantly asks, "Are you reading yet?" or similar questions that try to pinpoint your child's ability isn't being as helpful as she may suppose. Don't let your child think you're keeping track. Children are attuned to disappointment and worry in their parents' words and actions—even a well-meaning attitude of vigilance might end up supporting the opposite of what you want, with your child avoiding books so as not to let you down. And meanwhile, at this age there are many great books to read *together*! Marvel at them, laugh and cry your way through them. Enjoy every page. If you're doing all or the bulk of the reading for now, so be it.

### Remember Your Role

Reading at home should be about curiosity, discovery, and exploration. It's great, of course, to support your child while she's learning the mechanics of reading at school, but your most important job is more profound: to foster a *love* of reading. So leave the lessons to the classroom; don't put it on yourself to make your child hit particular targets. Your job is to make this a pleasure.

### Stay Faithful to Your Read-Aloud Routine

Be aware, too, that the transition from being read to to reading on your own is a big one, and for a lot of kids it can be emotionally fraught. Whatever your child's age when she starts to read all on her own—whether she's an early reader at 4 or a later one at 7—don't abruptly withdraw your reading services. Just as you don't stop hanging out in the pool with your child just because she's learned to swim, stick around when she's reading on her own. Being read to is a real comfort and part of your bond, and you don't want to convey to your child that becoming an independent reader jeopardizes that together time. If you hear your child begging to be read to, listen and obey. She is telling you she still wants and needs you to be involved in her story time. Remember, reading isn't just about absorbing words on your own—there's a whole gestalt you're fostering in your family's life. There's nothing wrong (far from it!) with continuing to read aloud those picture book favorites, and introducing new ones, even as your child begins to dazzle you with her feats of independent reading.

### Bring on the Classics

Regardless of where your child's independent reading is, the span between 4 and 8 is also a good time to start reading aloud more sophisticated books that he may not be able to read on his own yet but that will surely stimulate and enchant. Think about literary classics like Roald Dahl's *Charlie and the Chocolate Factory* or E. B. White's *Charlotte's Web*, as well as newer books like Kate DiCamillo's *The Miraculous Journey of Edward Tulane*. Reading these kinds of stories to children at this age may be one of the most satisfying reading experiences of your reading life. They don't have to know the meaning of every word to appreciate it. You will find yourself marveling all over again at their beauty and depth, and hearing the grace and perfection of the language makes a lasting impression on young ears. A book like *Through the Looking-Glass*, with its sophisticated wordplay and puzzles, is even better when shared with a favorite grown-up.

## You and Me, Me and You

As you're reading out loud, see if your emerging reader wants to take a shot at it. At first, you can point to individual words you know your child will recognize and have him read them. Eventually, once you can tell that your child is comfortable reading simple sentences, you can gently begin to share the stage during reading time. You can try reading aloud and alternating pages. Many books for new readers seem designed to make this kind of turn-taking fun, like Mo Willems's genius Elephant & Piggie books; you can each "play" one of the two friends, perhaps with full-body acting out. Making this work can depend on how diplomatically—even playfully—you phrase your request. Instead of saying, "Let me hear you read this last section to me," say, "I'd love for *you* to read *me* part of the story," or "Now it's Daddy's turn to listen."

When he *does* read out loud, listen respectfully, don't interrupt, and try to hold back on correcting him unless it's absolutely crucial to understanding the story. Montessori teachers have a great saying: "Teach, don't correct." You may think your small corrections are helping, but what you may end up doing is tamping down on early enthusiasm and barely budding confidence.

## Don't Harp

At 7, Maria's third child was still asking to be read to every night and resisting the old "you read one page, I read one page" routine that had been in place at that age with his older brother and sister. When he did take a turn reading, it went slowly—he seemed to be trudging ahead, without enjoyment. Finally, he was able to articulate the problem: "I hate reading out loud." Consider that possibility if your child is resisting reading to you.

You don't need to leap to the conclusion that he's having trouble read-ing on his own. Reading aloud is *not* the be-all and end-all. Some kids feel self-conscious. Others feel slowed down; when you think about it, you can read faster in your head, and some kids who may have trouble pronouncing everything aloud can move along far more quickly on their own.

It's also okay to have your own limits on reading out loud to children who can read themselves, as on everything else. Maria will confess to saying, some nights, to that 7-year-old son, "I literally can't keep my eyes open. Please can you read a page?" And he did.

### Keep Reading the Pictures

To encourage reading—without pressure!—give your child lots of books and other reading material that is heavily illustrated—and even wordless. It might seem a bit paradoxical, but as your child approaches the moment of learning to read words and crosses over into independent reading, images and pictures of all kinds are more important than ever. Teachers call this "visual reading." We hear often that our culture is increasingly visual—there's lots of information we've become used to seeing presented graphi-cally, with few or no words, like an airplane safety card or the instructions for assembling your Ikea dresser. But being able to follow a sequence of images is not just important to functioning in today's world—it's also a crucial stage in learning to read. Decoding, interpreting, and evaluating what's going on in a picture or a diagram or a visual narrative helps develop the parts of the brain that your child will be using to read words and sentences.

As your child enters first grade, which typically means more structured academic work at school, picture books can take on an especially impor-tant role. A picture book that tells its story or shares its knowledge through words and big, beautiful art is a salve to the soul of a child who is likely asked to work on dismal-looking photocopied worksheets all day long. Likewise, longer books that have a healthy ratio of illustrations to words are a gift even as your child gets more and more confident with reading.

Think about it: Pretty much everyone craves and appreciates the "break" illustrations give us from deciphering the words in long stretches of text and the extra information they offer—facial expressions, body lan-guage, visual jokes.

## Think Comics

Along with picture books, early readers, and, in time, chapter books, look for the latest comics and graphic novels created just for emerging readers. A book with fewer words and more pictures can be just as "advanced" as its text-heavy counterpart—especially these days, when the quality and richness of comics and graphic novels made for kids is sky-rocketing. Today's comics-style books have moved far beyond the realm of superheroes and silly, gross-out humor. In fact comics—whether classics like Peanuts or newer efforts featuring space explorers or just regular kids—can be a superb way for your child to learn to read and to learn to love reading.

What's more, many of the best picture books and "early readers" today are influenced by a comics style, using speech bubbles and panels on their pages. Some publishers focused on emerging readers are going all-in with the comics format. The early readers published by Toon Books, for example, are designed specifically to foster reading with comics-style layouts, which helpfully break up text and pictures into easy-to-follow panels, the story physically laid out step by step on the page into easily digestible portions.

## A New Reader, Out in the World

Your emerging reader is ready to be initiated into some of the pleasurable rituals around reading and books. If a favorite author is coming to your area for a reading and signing at a local bookstore or library, make every effort to bring your fan to meet her and see her in action. Turn it into a big to-do for the family or a special one-on-one outing. At this stage, meeting an author in real life can have an incredibly galvanizing effect, especially on a kid who's struggling a bit to get the hang of reading on his own. Authors will often talk about their process at a reading, which can help a child better understand and appreciate the art of the story. A personally signed book can be a lifelong treasure and can cement a permanent emotional relationship with that author, who enters a kind of mythical realm for the child. It's distinctly possible that after meeting an author and seeing him perform, your child will end up wanting every single book that person has written.

### Afternoon Entertainment

You may be surprised by how much you, too, enjoy an outing to see a kid's author in action. A little secret of the children's-books world is that many authors and illustrators are not getting by on selling books alone—they make a living by doing paid school, library, and bookstore visits, and they've really upped their game as performers. It goes without saying that these authors and illustrators are great with kids, but they always throw in a little something for the grown-ups, too. An experienced children's-book creator can make a multigenerational audience laugh, cry, and feel excited about their talent, versatility, and big, generous hearts.

### For the Love of Books

At this stage, it's important to keep sprinkling the fairy dust around reading and books whenever you see an opportunity. There are many ways to convey to your child how much you value books. Carefully gift wrap books you are giving to others. Ooh and ahh over them. Show your own excitement when a sequel comes out that you've been dying to read, or when your name comes up on the library waitlist for the latest prize-winning novel. At the dinner table, make "what you're reading" as regular a part of conversation as what you're watching on TV or what happened that day at the office. Become a fountain of positive vibes and good conversation about individual books and reading in general. This kind of enthusiasm is flat-out contagious, and can help carry an emerging reader through this period he may find challenging.

### Getting Started on Social Reading

Not surprisingly, as children begin to develop real social relationships, many of them want to read what their friends are enthusiastic about. When you're with your child and a friend, ask the friend, "What are you reading?" Start a conversation about the book: Why does he like it? What's the best part so far? Ask other parents what *their* children are reading, and track those books down. Offer to swap books. You're helping your child build conversations and friendships around books and shared experiences.

## A Big-Kid Thing

You can also make it clear to your child that reading is associated with maturity. Reading is quite a grown-up pastime, after all. It can be private or even secret. If your child's bedtime is seven o'clock, offer an extended thirty minutes of quiet bedtime reading to be used only if he wants to stay in bed and read. This turns reading into a privilege—something big kids "get" to do rather than something that "has" to be done. Otherwise, it's lights out at seven o'clock sharp.

When you're in the library or bookstore together, consider allowing your child to wander around the confines of the children's section without you trailing behind. Let her make her own discoveries. She chooses, she decides. You can keep one eye on her whereabouts, if it makes you more comfortable, but make it clear to your child that now that she's becoming a reader, you're happy to see her off on her own, following her own interests— just as you do.

## Discretion, the Better Part of Valor

You can be aware of the "reading level" of the books you steer your emerging reader toward—many books published specifically for this stage make it easy for you, with numbers or letters emblazoned on the cover to tell you what level they are intended for—but keep that information to yourself. You really shouldn't talk about books in terms of how "easy" or "hard" they are, or what number or letter is on their covers. It can feel like a judgment or grading, especially if the grades seem not so good. (Never compare your child's reading level with that of another child.)

If your approach to books at this stage is geared to getting your child to climb some ladder of achievement in reading, he will quickly figure that out, and you risk turning him off to the whole notion of a pleasure delivery system. Remember: He will learn to read fluently when the time is right. For you the more important question is, will he *want* to?

### The Competitive Element

Unfortunately, reading has become a competitive sport at many schools, with classrooms that are full of overt and subtle indicators of your child's success in mastering reading, like teacher-chosen reading groups that identify which kids are "better" at reading. It's likely your child knows exactly where he stands in relation to his classmates. It may in fact be making him sad or stressed, or if he's higher up the hierarchy, tempting him to be boastful or gloating. If you suspect that's the case, make it your job to defuse competition, reassure, encourage, and boost. Your child may not read fluently, but perhaps he reads with expression. Perhaps he chooses books you especially love—he's got great taste. Point out what he's good at.

Instead of telling her a book is "easy" or "hard" enough, talk about a book's subject or story. You can talk about whether it's a good book that you heard a lot of kids like. You can mention how funny it is, or point out how beautiful the art is, or observe that the girl in the story loves gorillas, just like she does.

### On the Other Hand

If your child is reading at a high level, tearing through books that are well past the reach of her peers, she may still face some specific, and perhaps surprising, challenges. For one thing, a child may read the words and sentences of a book fluently while not being able to fully understand the story. Learning to read actually consists of two separate elements: the mechanics of "decoding" the letters and words, and the process of being able to follow a story or information presented sequentially. Often these two processes don't click into place at the same time, and if a child is reading all the words of a book without really following what's going on, she still has a way to go in the process of becoming a reader.

### Keeping It Comprehensible

With a fast, strong reader who is, say, barely 6 years old, keep an eye out for books that she can actually understand and appreciate. It may be that your kindergartner can read books written with a 9-year-old audience in mind, but what is she getting out of them? Is she missing much of the nuance, the humor, the details of emotional experiences for which she has no context? That may be unavoidable, and it can be a problem if you think she's reading books that are somehow inappropriate or upsetting. Those books may be better suited for her when she's older. Look over what she's getting her hands on, of course, and be available to discuss them—or even encourage her to wait to read certain books, with the idea that she'll enjoy them more in, say, third grade, when she's closer to the age of the characters. And keep in mind that some of the books she's finishing now, she should revisit later, when she can understand more of the book's whole picture.

### Aging the Character

One rule of thumb says that kids like to read about kids their age or just slightly older, but there are enough exceptions to this rule to make us think twice about using it as a blanket guideline. Ramona, for example, is a kindergartner, but those Beverly Cleary books are better suited for first, second, or even third graders who enjoy feeling slightly superior to the occasionally clueless and misunderstood youngest child on Klickitat Street.

If you have a child who reads well and with great comprehension at an early age, you can enrich that experience by complimenting her when she does well on some aspect that isn't her specialty: reading a book outside her wheelhouse, slowing down while reading aloud, helping a struggling younger sibling recognize her letters. As with everything, children especially benefit from helping and teaching others. (It may also prevent her from becoming insufferable.) And keep encouraging her to reach new heights. If she's in second grade, you might give her a book you loved in third grade. You can even inscribe it and give it as a gift because you "think she's ready for it." Tell her you can't wait to talk to her about the wise heroine, or find out what she thinks of the ending.

### The Exceptional Mr. Potter

We love Harry Potter, and one of the things we love best about the series is that although many teens and adults are nuts for the books, J. K. Rowling wrote them for children in the second through sixth or seventh grades. It's turned out that the Potter phenomenon is so power-ful, younger kids want a piece of the action, too. Our advice is this: Don't push Harry Potter too early. We both experienced the "My kindergartner is reading Harry Potter" boast as competitive parental sport. Everyone seemed to know at least one kid who'd plowed his way through the series by first grade. Or whose parents played it on audio in the car. Or who read the entire series to their child who couldn't read it on his own yet. If that made everyone happy—great.

But even the first Harry Potter book is not necessarily appropriate for an emerging reader to read on her own. And there are some mature and extremely dark themes in the later books that could genuinely freak out a younger kid (like innocent children dying, teenage romance, puberty, and betrayal); J. K. Rowling wrote those with the understanding that her readers would grow into the later books as they worked their way through the series.

When you're deciding when to give the Potter books to your child (assuming it's even *your* choice), consider waiting until she is fully able to read and appreciate the books independently. Kids really don't need you in the driver's seat for the lifetime ride that Harry Potter can turn out to be. For many, it's something that will not only be an enthralling reading experience but will become a big part of their very identity for years to come. Maria's daughter, at 15, was still identifying herself as a Slytherin, right along with all the other interests and passions that make up who she is. It's also perfectly fine if your child never gloms on to the Potter phenomenon. Some children don't like fantasy; others reject books they think are overhyped. Some kids—Maria has one of these, too—find the books boring. Others find them too scary, no matter the age. There are many other great books out there. Let children have their own preferences.

### What If My Child Isn't Reading Yet?

Let's pause here to reiterate a simple, eternal fact: Learning to read can be hard. It doesn't come easily for many kids, and the process, espe-cially at a young age or before the child's individual brain is entirely ready to read, can be frustrating. Parents often feel under a lot of pressure

## When to Consult an Outside Expert

What if your child still trips over letters in first grade? What if your kid refuses to even try reading? These are legitimate concerns that might indicate a problem that can be solved with the help of a professional.

Be aware that kids with reading problems can be very good at hiding the real source of their struggle. Consider every possible obstacle your child could be up against in deciphering those letters and attaching them to sounds. The answer might surprise you—her slowness to read could be caused by a vision or hearing problem, for example, one she may have quite masterfully diverted attention from. Some kids can even game vision and hearing tests, especially if they are done at school or in a clinic and they're able to see

or hear other kids taking those same tests. Even children with clear cases of dyslexia become adept at covering up their difficulties.

Once you've ruled out more physical problems like those, you should begin by talking with your child's teacher or the school's reading specialist— almost all elementary schools now have a teacher on staff or on call who is specifically trained to spot and help correct reading challenges that are neurological or cognitive. If you think the school does not offer strong enough resources for struggling readers, a private reading specialist can help you find out if a developmental or learning issue is at work. If you are concerned, there is no harm, and a huge opportunity to help, in flagging the issue early on and checking in with an expert.

themselves—whether from their own parents ("But *you* were reading at that age!"), judgmental fellow parents around the classroom, well-intentioned teachers, or just good old-fashioned parental worry. It's also really hard to watch your child struggle and to see her overcome with frustration.

### Multilingual Challenges

The leap into reading is especially tough when it comes to English language books, because English is a particularly challenging language to master. Ask anyone who has learned English as a second language about the perils of phonetics, and you'll immediately hear about how difficult it is compared with Spanish or German or French, where, for example, the suffix *-eux* always sounds the same. Compare it with *-ough*, which can sound entirely different, depending on whether the word is *through* or *though* or *tough*. If English isn't your own first language or the language your partner grew up speaking, you may feel like supporting your child is extra difficult as well. Sensitivity and patience are key.

### Eyes on the Prize — Enjoyment

What the teacher does in the classroom may be beyond your control. She may be under pressure from state-mandated standards, curriculum guidelines, or demands from administrators and school board members. What *is* under your control is how reading is approached in your home, where you can keep the focus on excitement, enjoyment, appreciation, and enthusiasm rather than plowing grimly through a book that frustrates your struggling reader.

As your children approach the independent reading stage, it's likely you'll encounter some tricky or sensitive situations. Handling some of these will require nothing more complicated than emotional support or gentle empathy. If your son is embarrassed that all his friends are already reading, or if your daughter makes fun of her little sister's inability to master Dr. Seuss, remind them that every child learns different tasks at different ages. You may point out that the younger sibling learned to tie his shoes earlier than all his friends or that he's excelling at the activites in Scouts. You may also pull out that famous story about Albert Einstein's delayed speech, Theodore Roosevelt's many childhood illnesses, or other instances of late bloomers who later soar. You can explain to them that earlier and faster is not always better, and that strengths develop over the long term.

### Build in Success

Read aloud a rhyming book—one of Bill Peet's rhyming stories or a favorite Dr. Seuss—and leave out the rhyming word for your child to fill in. Is he reading it? Is he guessing it? Is he playfully suggesting a word he knows isn't actually on the page? Doesn't matter. It's fun and it's reading, in its way. And you can persuasively appreciate the result with a clap or a laugh, whichever the case calls for.

## Even Excellent Learners Can Struggle

Picking up reading can be hard for even the brightest child because of a specific challenge such as dyslexia. Or reading difficulties might be one of a constellation of issues that form a larger picture, like auditory processing disorder or autism spectrum disorder. If your child is facing one of those challenges, early intervention can make a big difference. Because the way children with dyslexia or other challenges learn to read is different from how other students do, it makes sense to get the appropriate kind of instruction rather than to toil fruitlessly using methods that probably don't work as well. The young brain is extremely elastic, and altering certain patterns is often far easier at a young age, before they've become ingrained.

If it turns out your child has a reading problem, there's no reason to despair. Some incredibly accomplished authors struggled with dyslexia as children. Those who struggle at first to get the hang of reading are just as likely as anyone else to go on to become excellent readers. This was the case for a 12-year-old boy named Josh, who lives in Florida and told his inspiring story to Maria: "I am a dyslexic and I spent about three years of my life learning the letters and practicing reading. Now just knowing that I can read is so amazing, because I remember when I couldn't, and it was so sad. Some kids would tease me. It just wasn't fun. So my mom got me help and I became an excellent reader, and ever since, I've really loved to read. I usually read whatever I can get my hands on. It's been like a miracle." It's also comforting—and a massive pressure release—for a child who feels different or stupid to be surrounded by other kids who are struggling in the same way.

### Gamify the Experience

Take turns with speaking the words of two different characters. Take turns reading pages with a twist: If your child is on the left, he reads the left page. If the left page ends up being extra wordy, don't fuss if he asks you to "switch" pages for a turn. Ask him to tell the story through pictures, while you tell it through words. If it's a comic, he does the speech bubbles while you handle the more onerous captions. This is especially great with books that have lots of "booms" and "arghs." Playing around a bit makes reading not only a shared experience but also a *fun* one.

### Note Your Mistakes and Embrace Theirs

All of us occasionally trip over words or garble something when reading aloud (especially tired parents). Note when you make a mistake and don't make a big deal out of it. This lets your child see that even grown-ups and fluent readers make mistakes when reading—that nobody reads perfectly even when they "know how." Laugh at your own silly syntax. Let your child laugh at you, too. This creates a forgiving atmosphere in which his reading stumbles won't stand out as some form of tragedy. Seek out some of the many books for emerging readers that show mistakes as something inevitable and even useful, like *Beautiful Oops!* by Barney Saltzberg, *Ish* by Peter H. Reynolds, and *The Book of Mistakes* by Corinna Luyken.

### The First Library Card

A child's first library card represents a rite of passage, and it is often the very first official membership card in a young life. Many libraries don't have a minimum age requirement, so help your child acquire the card at a time when it can have an effect. Teach your children that library membership is a privilege and a responsibility. Most children really treasure their library cards, for good reason. It's not just a ticket to great books; it's a milestone. For many, it's the first card in their first wallet.

### Ways to Praise

Even if the words don't come easily, praise the emotion, the fact that he's narrating aloud, his interpretation of the stories or the pictures, his enthusiasm. This helps alleviate the anxiety and builds confidence, even when your child is obviously struggling.

### Think Twice About Your Language

Ask your child to read a story *with* you, not to read *to* you. Small tweaks to your language can shift the dynamic. It's the difference between "Time to practice your violin" and "Would you give me a little violin concert?" or "Grandma is dying to hear the new piece you learned in piano." Pressure can be lifted just as easily as it can be applied.

### Listen to a Story, Watch a Story

Audiobooks are a godsend for many kids with dyslexia or other reading challenges. Not being able to physically read a book doesn't mean you don't enjoy stories or appreciate a good narrative. Audiobooks are especially great at teaching everything else literature brings us: nuanced characters, interesting word choices, complex sentence structure, engrossing plots. Your child can learn to love literature by listening to books so that once he *is* able to read those books himself, he'll be extra good at understanding them. And he'll get to enjoy them until that time comes. Many printed books come with audio accompaniment so that kids can try to read along as they listen. Also, Scholastic offers a number of great picture books on video, often with subtitled captions to help children read along as they watch. You can also find videos of loads of books read aloud on YouTube. Is all this exactly the same as reading a book entirely on your own? No, but for a child who is struggling, they can make a meaningful difference.

## What to Look For: Books for Emerging Readers

### Fun. Adventure. Playfulness.

Books labeled or conceived of as "early readers" allow children to enter their own personal world of books. That's a leap filled with prestige and accomplishment, but it shouldn't be daunting, and it definitely should not be boring. Find early readers that surprise and delight, even in their simplicity. Dr. Seuss revolutionized this category and set the standard that still holds. An early reader book should make reading seem like a club your child wants to be a part of—not a lesson to be graded on.

### Rhyme

Many early readers use rhyme—it's a way to give a fledgling reader a clue about what an unfamiliar word may be—but an early reader doesn't have to rhyme to be great. Repetition and word patterning can be just as helpful. Early readers can even get into wordplay and punning. Even the most basic learn-to-read books, like Scholastic's bestselling Bob Book series, can offer humor and goofy rhymes.

### Eye on Art and Design

The art on every page of an early reader should help the child decode the words; a good early reader establishes a clear relationship between illustration and text. Make sure these books have an inviting design. Many of the best early readers have very few words—sometimes only one or two per page. Remember, much of the point of these books is to help the child make it through sequential narratives of increasing complexity—following the steps of the story is the point, as much as decoding the words. Rest assured, your child is reading when making it through a book with very few words. It is a satisfying and impressive accomplishment to finish each and every one of those books on one's own.

### Clever Picture Book/Early Reader Hybrids

Many of the best early readers do double duty as picture books. You may even have already read them aloud to your toddler or preschooler—think of classics like the Frog and Toad or George and Martha books. A look at recent winners and runners-up of the Theodor Seuss Geisel Award, given by the American Library Association to "the most distinguished American book for beginning readers," is instructive. We could have sworn that some of these gems were straight-up picture books: Kevin Henkes's *Waiting*, Laura Vaccaro Seeger's *First the Egg*, and Jon Klassen's *I Want My Hat Back*, for example. But they are also ideal for a kid who's turning pages all on her own.

# Be Wary Of

. . . . . . . . . . . . . . . . . . . .

### "Leveled" Early Reader Books

These educational-looking books use a limited number of words and are heavily illustrated. Most have a more workmanlike appearance than picture books. They may have no jacket and be slightly taller and narrower; they are often available in paperback and may be displayed on a spinning rack in the store. Many are branded with names like "I Can Read" or "Step into Reading," with three or sometimes four levels. These are called "leveled readers"—you can always spot one because it will have a giant number or letter on the cover identifying its level. Your child is likely to encounter these in school, starting in kindergarten. For that reason, we both shied away from bringing branded "leveled reader" books home. There are plenty of early reader books that don't create the pressured atmosphere those numbers can convey.

### Books That Look "Babyish"

Especially if your emerging reader is on the older side, beware of early readers that seem geared to a younger child's sensibility, whether in the look of the illustrations or the topic. These may make him feel awkward and embarrassed about where he is with his reading skills. Does he feel he has outgrown talking vehicles or barnyard-animal shenanigans? Be sensitive to that. A better choice might be an early reader with a strong comic-book look and sensibility, or a book of nonfiction fun facts.

### Grandma's Early Readers

You know these when you see them, whether at a sidewalk sale or on a shelf in that frozen-in-time summer house you're renting: books from the "Dick and Jane" era of early readers in which everything, from the language to the illustrations of the children themselves, was somehow both stiff and cutesy (and the world apparently consisted only of white people, mostly blond). These can be amusing for adults, but no child today should have to learn to read with them.

# Our Picks for Emerging Readers

### One Fish Two Fish Red Fish Blue Fish
**Dr. Seuss**

With its zippy rhymes and zany parade of unusual-looking creatures ("Not one of them is like another. Don't ask me why. Go ask your mother"), this one puts a smile on the grumpiest face, every time.

### Waiting Is Not Easy!
**Mo Willems**

Impatient Gerald has to wait for Piggie's promised surprise. Every book in the Elephant & Piggie series is an example of genius, but this one may be our favorite. Oh, wait—there's also the series's grand finale, *The Thank You Book*. That one is *also* our favorite.

### Little Mouse Gets Ready
**Jeff Smith**

A fantastic, funny book for a child who has taken the first steps toward reading words on her own. Little Mouse works so hard to get dressed and then makes a hilarious discovery at the end. (Spoiler alert: Mice don't wear clothes!)

### Ball, Treat, AND Frankie
**Mary Sullivan**

These books look like picture books, but they are perfect as the very first books with words a child reads—they use only two or three words throughout, with a stories that are clever, fun, and easy to follow, making them a thrill for the newest readers.

### Dog and Bear series
**Laura Vaccaro Seeger**

A stuffed bear and a real dachshund are the best of friends in Seeger's clever, adorable series. Each book brings together three very brief stories in which the two pals barely leave the house but still have satisfying adventures.

### A Friend for Dragon
**Dav Pilkey**

Dragon is blue, round, and not at all ferocious—in fact, he's kind and quite dim, which makes you want to protect him from all the trouble that finds him in this sweet, funny book. What he needs most is something that is sometimes difficult to get hold of: a friend.

## Barkus
**Patricia MacLachlan,**
**illustrated by Marc Boutavant**
In easy-to-read and almost hypnotically appealing language, MacLachlan presents a series of surprises for her plucky little red-haired narrator, starting with the arrival of a super-fun dog who names himself Barkus. Boutavant's whimsical, graphically interesting art makes Barkus's adventures a candy-colored delight.

## Tales for the Perfect Child AND Fables You Shouldn't Pay Any Attention To
**Florence Parry Heide**
**and Sylvia Worth Van Clief,**
**illustrated by Sergio Ruzzier**
These ultra-short, ultra-witty tales of naughty children and badly behaving animals won a cult following when they first appeared in the 1980s, with art by Victoria Chess. Now they've been reissued with wily new art by Sergio Ruzzier that perfectly suits their offbeat sensibility.

## George and Martha
**James Marshall**
These sneakily funny classics could be considered picture books, but a fledgling reader will especially appreciate spending time with  these two hippo friends who try so hard to be nice to each other and have a hard time figuring out how to do that.

## Frog and Toad series
**Arnold Lobel**
The books in Lobel's series from the 1970s are still beloved, with their warm depiction of the devoted bond between worrywart Toad and magnanimous Frog, who might appear similar but are polar opposites in temperament. Read aloud or on a child's own, they satisfy.

# THE INDEPENDENT
# READER

Independence! Arriving there after inevitable struggles and near misses is exciting to children in every area of life, from walking to wearing underwear to bike riding, and reading is no exception. For parents, watching your child become an independent reader may be especially sweet. Now she is really entering the larger world, the world of letters, the place where we all coexist and communicate, hash out our differences, and set loose our dreams.

So, what happens now? When children are flowing right through their early readers, they may start to talk about chapter books. If not, introduce the idea yourself—they're probably ready or will be soon. For many kids, chapter books beckon like gleaming trophies after the slog of the early reader period. Something about the feat of working through a bunch of chapters makes a young elementary school student feel amazingly grown-up. Take time to recognize the accomplishment. Now you have a tangible reward to offer: better books or at least books without ages and stages stamped on their covers. The books even start to look like more fun. And these new books will provide your child with his own private experience, with stories targeted to his comprehension level and interests. Consider this a blessing. Many chapter books for this age group may seem simple, formulaic, and, to adult minds at least, stultifying. That said, the main "work" the kids are doing at this stage is *just* figuring out their preferences and opinions, and honing in on what they love in a book.

## Here's What You Need to Know

### Submit to the Series

It is a truth universally acknowledged that a child in possession of the ability to read must be in want of a series. Why fight it? Series take up the majority of shelf space devoted to newly independent readers in libraries and bookstores. Familiar franchises like Magic Treehouse, Flat Stanley, and Fancy Nancy are among them. Some of these series have installments counting into the hundreds. Explore the available books, and steer your child to a series you think brings a little extra pizzazz to the table. We suggest mainly stocking up at the library or buying just a few and then swapping with friends, since each book is usually read once and only once.

### A World of Choice

Both of us—and our children—are partial to series aimed at newly independent readers that are heavily illustrated, like Bad Kitty, Dory Fantasmagory, and Andy Griffiths's 13- (and 26-, and so on) Story Treehouse books. Now is also a good time to give them an occasional blast from the past—vintage series, like the A to Z Mysteries or the Encyclopedia Brown mysteries and eventually Nancy Drew, that will let them visit an exotic past and see how much the world has changed—and hasn't.

### Series Attachment

At some point during the early chapter book stage, a certain series may exert a tenacious hold on your child. Just as babies like routines, young children crave familiarity in terms of characters, story line, and resolutions. Much of their world is changing at a rapid clip; they can find comfort relying on recognizable patterns. Still, you can add some variety. Just because they love mysteries now doesn't mean they won't also love funny animal stories or school tales, in the same way adult readers can appreciate science fiction even if their core passion is poetry. Think of what your child *isn't* being exposed to in her classroom or favorite bookstore or older brother's shelf. Open those literary landscapes to her.

### Keep Picture Books in the Picture

First-time parents get used to saying goodbye to entire stages of their small child's life that simply and unequivocally come to an end: the Peekaboo Period, the Stroller Years. . . . But here is something that may come as a surprise: When it comes to books, with a few exceptions, a child is never really too old for anything. That goes double and triple for picture books. They are not just an art form that speaks to everyone; many of them are lifelong favorites well worth revisiting again and again—starting now, when your child is beginning to read on her own. Also, remember that, with the assumption a parent will be reading them aloud, many picture books contain more sophisticated language than your newly independent reader can handle at this point; a reader who can manage "higher" level books on his own may still have trouble reading certain picture books himself. These days, we are also seeing more and more picture books specifically aimed at readers in the later elementary or even early middle-school years, so be aware that while it may look from afar like a cousin of *Where the Wild Things Are*, it may actually be a biography intended for fourth to eighth graders.

### Young at Heart

Along these lines, if your child is interested in something that to you seems "young" for where you know he is reading-wise, hold back on any judgment or even an opinion. There may be some specific aspect of that book that is speaking to your child. Or maybe he just feels like reading something less obviously challenging at the moment (just like grown-ups sometimes do). Many children have "comfort books" that they return to often as the years go by. Even for kids, "the reading life" is a big and very personal picture. How great that your child is already asserting her own needs and preferences through books.

For another thing, kids absolutely love to revisit books they read when they were "little." In both of our families, the older kids would often sneak in and grab a picture book they heard being read aloud to a younger sibling so they could enjoy it in privacy on their own. Or they would take temporary possession of new picture books that came into the house, just to "check out" what the little one was up to. So once the chapter book years are in full swing, don't throw away *all* the old "younger" books. Go ahead and pass those "I Can Read" books down to a younger sibling or cousin or friend, but do not abandon all the glorious picture books of early childhood. Even if your child asks to get rid of them or derides them as "baby" books, hold back on giving these treasures the boot. That child will sing a different song in a few years.

### Read to Your Big Kid

Picture books aren't the only relics from early childhood to hold on to— also try to retain a regular read-aloud time. Although it's inspiring to see your child read on his own, kids (and, come on, grown-ups, too) still appreciate the snuggle-in time of bedtime storytelling. This is yet another benefit of establishing a habit of reading out loud to your kids early on. As they approach and enter the tween years, with all the new social pressure, bodily changes, and expectations from their teachers, it can become hard to ask a parent for a simple hug. But they need warm physical contact now as much as ever. Many of the other moments of physical comfort that younger children enjoy with their parents have gone away, from zippering a jacket to clipping fingernails. It's not so long until you, too, will miss that ready access to hugs and snuggles, so take advantage. Just find that comfortable balance between the time your child spends reading on his own and the time you read together. A ratio of about half and half until age 8 is one good guideline, but it will no doubt vary from kid to kid and even at different times of the year.

### Character Connection

Be on the lookout for books to bring home that will connect to your reader right where he is—not just as a reader but as a human being. There are books that address nearly every milestone, occasion, worry, fear, goal, and interest. When it's springtime, you can find great books about nature, trees, gardens, animals, and the outdoors. When summer rolls around, there are sports books, adventure tales, camp stories. At back-to-school time, you might suggest *Anne of Green Gables*. When a book helps introduce a subject or illuminate a topic or answer a burning question, children learn that books are a place to turn for enhancing and enriching their lives. A book can offer a solution to many of life's predicaments, for children as well as adults. In many ways, every book is a kind of self-help book for kids. They anticipate concerns, answer questions, and solve nagging problems. And when children learn from an early age that books can do this for them, they never forget that lesson.

### The Classics Step Up

Reading classic novels aloud is a fun way to introduce some of the all-time greats of children's literature to kids reading confidently on their own, who might not otherwise pick up those books—or get as much out of them. Some of Pamela's kids' favorites were the Narnia books, Maud Hart Lovelace's old-timey Betsy-Tacy series, the Wizard of Oz books, *Alice's Adventures in Wonderland*, *The Hobbit* and *Lord of the Rings*, the Little House series, and *Treasure Island*. These books, with their occasionally intricate language, complicated story lines, and references to an earlier age, often beg for parental explanation. You'll have opportunities to discuss historical context, word definitions, and sophisticated themes—like the troubling treatment of Indians in the Little House books, and how much the world has changed since then. If your kids—like Maria's—balk at hearing the more antiquated language of certain classics, consider more accessible versions. Sharing Robert Sabuda's astonishing pop-up version of *Alice's Adventures in Wonderland* was a ton of fun, and an abridged version of the Wizard of Oz series enraptured them. As kids get older, they can return to reread all these books independently (and of course, will want to see all the related movies).

### Beyond Stories

Remember, too, that sharing books together doesn't always mean hunkering down with a traditional story for a hushed and intimate story time. A variety of books can open up fantastic conversations between

generations, and certain kinds are particularly suited for a looser kind of mutual enjoyment. Now that they can read, take advantage! Kids love sharing the crazy facts in books of records or believe-it-or-nots. They love compendiums of weird-but-true historical events. Comic books as well. Pamela probably has heard more Calvin and Hobbes comic strips read aloud than she's read on her own. Added incentive: These books are staples of yard sales and used-book sales. Poetry falls into this category, too. It's easily read aloud, enjoyed, shared, and memorized by listeners of all ages. Because so much poetry for children takes the form of nursery rhymes, chants, and songs, often infused with humor, a child's appreciation for verse can be encouraged from a very early age. By the time they're independent readers, poetry is just part of their regular reading diet.

### The Digital Behemoth

If you've been reading this book in order, you may have noticed, or rather not noticed, an elephant in the room. And not just any elephant. A gigantic, dangerously approachable, seductive and sneaky, multitentacled, and utterly mesmerizing beast. We're talking, of course, about the screens in our lives—the smartphones, tablets, TVs, game consoles, and laptops that are everywhere you look. They are everywhere your child is looking, too—even if you hold off from giving your children these tempting little objects yourself. How can we keep our children from becoming slaves to the screen? Now that they have learned to read, and even do it on their own, how can we be sure they're becoming lifelong readers when the current environment can seem so hostile to the very idea of sitting down quietly with an old-fashioned, turn-the-pages printed book?

## Book-Inspired Gifts

Jackie Kennedy famously created a wonderful family ritual for her children, Caroline and John, by asking them to forgo buying her gifts and instead asking them to give her a poem, whether it was one they wrote themselves, one they wrote out for her, or one they memorized and recited aloud. What a gift that was to her children as well! As your kids become independent readers—and writers—borrow that idea, use one of our suggestions below, or come up with your own book-inspired suggestions for gift giving. Of course, if you're lucky enough to get books as gifts, save them and bring them out again a few years later. Your children will be rewarded as much as you will.

- **Creative comics:** Comic books are simple enough for even very young children to write on their own. And some kids love the organizational joy of creating panels, drawing speech bubbles and simple characters and story lines.

- **Story-time coupons:** You know those Mother's Day "coupon" books that elementary school teachers sometimes ask students to create as gifts? Your child can create their own book-oriented coupons for you—where Daddy gets to pick the story to read that night, or your son will read aloud the book of your choice.

- **A vacation story:** Ask your child to write captions for the photos from a family vacation. She can pick which ones go in the album and in which order (sequencing!) and write the captions herself. For an especially "official-looking" product, this is easy to do with many photo websites and apps.

- **Mommy's biography:** Ask your child to write the story of your life, as he or she sees it. She can interview you about your childhood or your favorite books, and then write it up and give it to you as a present. Variations: Ask your child to write his own story. His grandfather's story. Or a story about both parents. If he's a fan of fairy tales or fantasy, suggest he do it in that genre.

### It Starts with You

We'll say it again, because it's easy to forget among the demands of parenthood: If you want your child to be excited about reading, you should be, too. Share with them how you *choose* to read books, despite the call of digital culture. Devices can be opaque (whereas a physical book is more transparent), so if you're reading a book on a device, read a few interesting lines of your book aloud to your child so he doesn't think you're just scrolling through Instagram. Tell him about a word you read that you had to look up because you didn't know the meaning. And even if you prefer reading your own books on a tablet, take care to read print books in front of your kid as often as you can—it's a visual message that has a lasting effect.

## Screen Stories

Lately, many clever picture books have taken on the subject of the tyranny of screens and the cultural onslaught of incessant entertainment. These are excellent choices to give to a kid who may be surrounded by screens and trying to figure out where reading actual books fits into it all. In *Hello! Hello!* by Matthew Cordell, a heroine ventures outdoors when her family is too glued to their screens to notice her. *On a Magical Do-Nothing Day* by Beatrice Alemagna celebrates the joy of exploring nature and embracing open-ended, screen-free leisure time by telling a story about the deep pleasure awaiting a kid "stuck" in a country house with no screen access. And the equally gorgeous *Blue Rider* by Geraldo Valério celebrates the enduring allure of print for a child surrounded by other people glued, soullessly, to screens. We feel certain there are more books like these to come!

## Small and Mighty

Those smaller screens are the hardest, but they are also the most important for parents to regulate, because they can seem so similar to books. They can even be, in the case of Kindles and other e-readers, book delivery systems, which is fine for many adults but not recommended for children, with their more vulnerable developing brains. Even if you've come to rely on the convenience of your Kindle, while your child is still a newly independent reader, and even right up until she becomes a teenager who may demand otherwise, always give her printed books to read rather than e-books. Studies have shown that children, even more than adults, absorb and retain stories better when they read them in print.

## Keep Screens Out of the Bedroom

At night, screen time is known to interfere with melatonin cycles, which makes it harder to fall asleep. For this reason alone, having screen-free bedrooms, at the very least after dinnertime, makes sense as a family rule. If your kids balk, share this research with them. In the meantime, reading books in bed is—as it has always been—an excellent prelude to sleep. Whether it's reading out loud together, your child reading on his own while you're elsewhere, or the two of you reading your own books separately, side by side, in her room, it pays to make the hour or so before bedtime sacrosanct book-reading time.

## A Cold, Hard Look at Your Home

If devices like smartphones, iPads, and laptops are everywhere, they can drown out the appeal of the awesome books you're bringing home. Besides, there is no real benefit from screen time for preteenagers, and there are plenty of downsides. Your kid will have his own device eventually, and most experts recommend putting it off as long as possible. Many parents of younger children are already taking steps to try to control the presence of the internet and social media in their child's life. A movement called "Wait Until 8th," for example, asks parents to band together to pledge to wait until eighth grade to give kids smartphones, the idea being that the less pressure from friends to be online all day long, the easier it will be for kids to forgo that. When it comes to raising a reader, we're convinced that the smaller the presence of the internet and the fewer screens in your home and your child's life, the better.

## Book in Hand

Keep focusing on squeezing in more reading time of your own. It's all too easy to carry your phone around like it's a life preserver and you're on a boat caught in a storm, or to get more absorbed in that Netflix series you're halfway through than the novel on your nightstand. Grab that novel and bring it to the kitchen to get a few pages in while you're making dinner, then throw it on the sofa so it can call out to you later, before the TV makes a claim for your attention. Kids can sniff out hypocrisy even from a young age, so if you're asking your daughter to read a book while you gaze at an iPad or keep putting down your book to peek at your phone, she *will* notice. In other words, take small steps of your own to give books a bit of a handicap in the battle for attention in your home. Everyone will be richly rewarded.

**The Family That Reads Together**

Just as younger children parallel play, older children parallel read. And reading together—separately—is a wonderful way to spend time in one another's company. Instead of organizing family leisure time around movies or video games, try a regular family reading time. As your children begin to choose their own books and read independently, they may be less inclined to talk to you about what they're reading—but if they're reading right next to you, you'll hear them laugh, exclaim, or give some other response, which gives you an opening to conversation. You'll find your kids piping up to tell about something really cool they just read or share why they're laughing so hard. "What's so funny?" is a question kids love to answer.

## Out in the World

Just as you did when they were babies and toddlers, keep books present when you leave the house. Taking a family trip? Ask your kids to pack their books. (For less enthused readers, shift the tone to make it feel more voluntary by saying, "I'm bringing X, Y, and Z to read—which books are you packing?") When you hit the beach or pool, stock your bag with something for you—and your child—to read. The stories they read on trips or even at the town pool on a lazy summer day will become part of their cherished memories. They'll begin to associate certain books with certain places. Consider, too, that your vacations and even weekend trips can easily be turned into no-screen zones. Rent a place that has no TV, or maybe you just happen to end up in a hotel room with a TV that is mysteriously not working, and the Wi-Fi is out, too! Aww, too bad. Good thing you have plenty of books.

## Book-Centric Habits and Routines

These tactics will pay off now, and perhaps even more later, in the teenage years, when video games, YouTube, social media, and texting come at your kids from every corner. For now, one of the best ways you can mount your defense against that onslaught is by staying current with the books— and more likely, the series—that are captivating readers of your child's age. Keep an eye on *The New York Times* children's bestseller lists. The series list will inevitably include ones that are popular among your child's peers. When a new book in the series comes out, get a copy for your child—and talk about how great it is that finally, the next book is here. Taking initiative like that can help give your kid a regular reminder that books are powerful, books are emotional, books help form bonds between friends. They can crack you up, they can mesmerize and thrill you and help you understand yourself. And how cool is it that you can take them anywhere, and they never need to be charged? Books link you to other people, without the stress over "likes" and "favorites." And right alongside those social superpowers, reading books can also remain an entirely private world, one just right for your child.

# What to Look For:
# Books for Independent Readers

### Chapter Books

Given that beginning-level chapter books are mostly published in series, how do you suss out the best ones or the ones your child will most strongly respond to? Keep in mind that some series are best read in order, but in other series, your child can jump in at any point. For example, if you spot a book in the Geronimo Stilton series that looks like it's far into the ongoing story of these particular characters but that hits on an interest of your child, by all means, bring it home. The authors of these books know how to make each one appropriate for either newcomers or longtime fans. They are written to be entered at any point, with quick summaries of key who-what-when-wheres in the opening chapters.

### All Hail Graphic Novels

For independent readers in the elementary school years, the increasing excellence of graphic novels and nonfiction is among the most important trends in recent children's literature. Many are just right for newly independent readers, from Charise Mericle Harper's Crafty Cat series, which deals with school jitters, to Ben Clanton's Narwhal and Jelly books, which address friendship, to Ashley Spires's goofball Binky the Space Cat series, to Jorge Aguirre and Rafael Rosado's mash-up fairy-tale-fantasy worlds, starting with *Giants Beware!* American schools are even coming around to the wisdom of using comics and graphic novels in the classroom, as schools in France have for nearly a century. Teachers and librarians are finding that their students demand them and come back for more. What could be bad about that? Graphic fiction and nonfiction are both an efficient way to deliver information and a way to keep the enthusiasm for reading high among more visually oriented kids. For children who may still be reluctant or put off by the seeming demands of reading big chunks of text, comics and graphic novels are an excellent way to segue into—and keep up—the habit of reading.

## Illustration Nation

There are also many books well suited for fledgling readers that are not quite graphic novels but still have at least one illustration per page, like Scholastic's Branches books for early chapter book readers, which include popular series like the creepy-fun Notebook of Doom books and Hilde Cracks the Case, featuring a delightful girl journalist-detective based on an actual child who started a newspaper in her Pennsylvania hometown and solved a murder mystery. These books may look young and/or the illustrations may seem unsophisticated, but don't underestimate them. The best are not only brilliant at capturing the attention of children who may be turned off by straight blocks of text but are also high on emotion, humor, and suspense, which sweeps kids up and inspires them to move along.

# Be Wary Of

## Cardboard Characters

Avoid characters that feel uninspired, though be careful not to assert your own values too much; many kids, after all, love a good antihero like the Wimpy Kid or Captain Underpants, and what you consider lame, they may find hilarious. That said, there are certain characters that just fall flat. Your child probably doesn't feel like a gender stereotype, so he or she probably doesn't want to read a story with a stereotypical character either. Keep an eye out for strong—yet nuanced—boy and girl characters that go beyond the cookie cutter.

## Franchise Fatigue

Minecraft, Pokémon, Lego, Shopkins—reading is probably not the first thing that springs to mind when you hear the names of these toy and entertainment juggernauts, and yet all of them publish related chapter book series. These can have a useful place in a young reader's repertoire— they may be great ways to lure a very wary reader or to reinforce the habit and fun of reading in a child who has fallen off reading—but they're not going to expand your child's intellectual horizons or expose him to rich, memorable language or inventive storytelling possibilities.

# Our Picks: Chapter Book Series

### Ivy + Bean
**Annie Barrows,**
**illustrated by**
**Sophie Blackall**
Two friends—who
never meant to
like each other—
share adventures.
The books are
fail-safe and
charming, as are the illustrations by
Caldecott Medalist Sophie Blackall.

### Dory Fantasmagory
**Abby Hanlon**
With illustrations on every page and a
lovable heroine with a wild imagination
that mixes her real life and her fantasy
world, this may be Maria's favorite
contemporary chapter book series.

### Bad Kitty
**Nick Bruel**
The Bad Kitty story originated as a
picture book of the same name, in which
a cat goes berserk—in alphabetical
order. Then came the series of antic,
laugh-out-loud chapter books with
graphic novel elements, perfect for kids
who fell in love with the picture books
and want more.

### Anna Hibiscus
**Atinuke,**
**illustrated by Lauren Tobia**
This joyful series about a little African
girl is a revelation—the books ring with
laughter even as they stab delicately

at your heart. Nigerian-born Atinuke
tells stories of a family with a Canadian
mother and an African father, and
Tobia's gentle illustrations bring life to
every encounter.

### The Ramona books
**Beverly Cleary**
These are still the gold standard. A
rambunctious little girl who can't help
but get in trouble. An older sister whose
patience is tried. A lovable gang of friends
on Klickitat Street. Many contemporary
series aimed at girls have tried to capture
Ramona's naughtiness without the
brattiness but have rarely succeeded.
What Ramona and her neighborhood
friends capture so well, for both boy
and girl readers (don't forget the Henry
Huggins books!), is that world in which
kids ran around outside after school—
free, independent, perhaps a little more
grown-up than the grown-ups themselves
realized.

## I Survived

**Lauren Tarshis**

This action-packed series of historical first-person narratives is full of adventure, with topics well suited to nonfiction-minded kids: Tsunamis, revolutions, shipwrecks, and other disasters keep the plots thrumming along.

## The Little Tim books

**Edward Ardizzone**

The Little Tim books were originally published in the 1930s, and they have aged wonderfully, with classic pen-and-ink and watercolor art and big, old-fashioned letters telling the tale of Little Tim, who stows away on a steamer and kicks off a life at sea, with occasional trips back to see his relieved (but understanding) parents.

## Jenny and the Cat Club

**Esther Averill**

These delightfully old-fashioned stories, which range in format from "I Can Read" (*Pickles the Fire Cat*) to early chapter book (*Jenny's Birthday Book*) to the older stories of Jenny and the Cat Club, follow the adventures of Jenny Linsky, a black cat, and her posse of New York City felines as they amble out of their apartments into wider territory, including a magical moment in Central Park when Jenny and her friends dance "The Sailor's Hornpipe."

## The Matter-of-Fact Magic books

**Ruth Chew**

Beginning with *The Wednesday Witch*, these stories feature a sister and brother pair who encounter magic in their otherwise reality-based midst. The fantasy is lighthearted and completely fright-free.

## Clementine

**Sara Pennypacker,**
**illustrated by Marla Frazee**

With her strong opinions and dislike of being bossed around, Clementine knows she is "the hard one" in her family. But following her from kindergarten through fourth grade in this witty, socially aware, and surprisingly touching series is wonderfully easy.

# Our Poetry Picks

### I'm Just No Good at Rhyming
**Chris Harris,**
**illustrated by Lane Smith**
These short, frisky, and funny poems, accompanied by Smith's whimsical illustrations, have even poetry-resistant children reading verse before they realize what they're doing.

### You Read to Me, I'll Read to You
**John Ciardi,**
**illustrated by Edward Gorey**
This oldie-but-goodie from the 1960s starts with a directive about who—parent or child—will read which poems to whom, making it a perfect option for new readers. They include concise, funny, memorable verses about subjects such as sharks, breakfast, a hot day, and a sad day, complemented by the legendary Gorey's dark, weird line drawings.

### The New Kid on the Block
**Jack Prelutsky,**
**illustrated by James Stevenson**
Clever, hilarious, right on target for elementary school kids—that describes pretty much everything by Jack Prelutsky, who has a good sense for where the silly meets the sublime in his multiple themed collections.

### A Child's Garden of Verses
**Robert Louis Stevenson**
There are many editions of this 1885 classic, so choose the one whose illustrations appeal most to you and your kids. We like the exquisite detail and retro-modern feel of the version by the contemporary illustrator Barbara McClintock.

### Revolting Rhymes
**Roald Dahl**
Delivers on the title. If you've got a Dahl fan in the family, don't forget this collection of nasty, funny, absurd little poems, mostly about hideously behaving creatures.

### Poetry for Young People: Langston Hughes
**edited by David Roessel and Arnold Rampersad,**
**illustrated by Benny Andrews**
This wonderful series has individual volumes devoted to many of the greats, from Emily Dickinson to Maya Angelou, but we are especially enamored of the one introducing children to the Harlem Renaissance legend Hughes, with art by the great painter Benny Andrews. This volume, like all of them, includes an introduction accessible to older elementary schoolers that explains Hughes's life and work, and a selection of his most unforgettable, emblematic poems, such as "A Dream Deferred."

## Mirror, Mirror: A Book of Reverso Poems
**Marilyn Singer,
illustrated by Josée Masse**

Singer coined the term *reverso poems* for poems that read the same up or down the page— the first line and the last line are the same, the second line becomes the penultimate line, and so on. Even a poetry skeptic will find mind-blowing fun following these two-sided poetic portraits of figures from Greek mythology.

## Poems to Learn by Heart
**edited by Caroline Kennedy,
illustrated by Jon J Muth**

The premise and execution of this book are especially brilliant. Memorizing poetry is one of the greatest ways for children to build their appreciation of it. This collection goes from easiest to most challenging and works well for kids of all ages.

## Forget-Me-Nots: Poems to Learn by Heart
**edited by Mary Ann Hoberman,
illustrated by Michael Emberley**

Hoberman is a former US Children's Poet Laureate, and her selections here are diverse and spot-on. There are verses by everyone from Robert Frost to contemporary powerhouses Nikki Grimes and Naomi Shihab Nye—all chosen with ease of memorization in mind.

## Where the Sidewalk Ends AND A Light in the Attic
**Shel Silverstein**

Silverstein is simply the master of the absurd, and as many parents can attest, these poems stay with you for a lifetime.

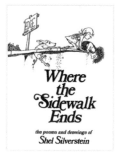

# PART THREE

# Your
# Middle-Grade
# Reader

# THE LEAP TO
# MIDDLE GRADE

By age 8, most kids are reading fluently on their own. This is when the next level of fun begins—they are officially readers of "middle-grade" books. It's just too bad the label *middle grade* doesn't sound fun at all. The term was created for the publishing industry and the educational system, where it's useful to set books for this age apart from simpler picture books or racier young adult (YA) novels. Hence that forbidding, institutional vibe. But "middle grade" is not the same as middle school (thankfully), nor is it really about grades or even ages. Middle-grade fiction is *children's literature*—books that we think of as "novels for children" in the broadest sense, the beloved classics both old and new, and the books that stay with us from childhood well into adulthood. *Charlotte's Web*, *The Phantom Tollbooth*, *A Wrinkle in Time* . . . these are middle-grade books.

It's at this point that children settle into the world of reading for true pleasure. They are now reading to become immersed in a story for hours on end, to discover new worlds, to acquaint themselves with fascinating

characters, people with lives different from their own. Reading these books, children discover who they themselves are. They find out more about subjects they're interested in. They are reading for the reasons all of us read: to escape, to uncover, to challenge ourselves, to be swept away by a compelling voice, to find companionship with characters we connect with, to travel the world from the safe distance of a living room armchair.

This makes the years your child is reading middle-grade books a great time for you, too. Not only is it gratifying to watch your child fall under the spell of great books all on his own, but you'll have the chance to redis-cover the children's novels you loved—and you'll likely find yourself falling for some new ones, too.

The standards you grew up on have been joined by a new wave of books that have inspired their own strong followings. The best of these books are so good—well written, exciting, heart wrenching—that parents will often find themselves reading them cover to cover, too. We're talking about novels like R. J. Palacio's *Wonder*, Peter Brown's *The Wild Robot*, Grace Lin's *Where the Mountain Meets the Moon*, and Jason Reynolds's Track series. And there's even more good news—a savvy new batch of authors has redefined what's possible when writing history or biography for chil-dren. Nonfiction has become as exciting for kids as fiction.

History books like Candace Fleming's *The Family Romanov: Murder, Rebellion, and the Fall of Imperial Russia*, Deborah Hopkinson's *D-Day: The World War II Invasion That Changed History* and Steve Sheinkin's *Bomb: The Race to Build—and Steal—the World's Most Dangerous Weapon* take the kind of subjects that kids used to encounter only in dry social studies textbooks and turn them into electrifying narrative nonfiction. They are written in clear, accessible language, with vivid storytelling and dramatic structure. These books are also generous with photography and other visuals, some-times featuring an image every couple of pages. Adults will quite possibly find themselves not only engaged, but gaining new understanding of a sub-ject like the Vietnam War after spending time with a book like *Vietnam: A History of the War*, by Russell Freedman, for instance.

We're also happy to note the advent of "Young Readers Editions" of bestselling or award-winning adult nonfiction books, like Tom Rinaldi's

*The Red Bandanna*, a moving 9/11 story, the ballerina Misty Copeland's autobiography, *Life in Motion*, or Michael Pollan's manifesto against processed food and corporate agriculture, *The Omnivore's Dilemma*. These books bring great nonfiction to curious children. Also—and this may shock you—compared with their original versions, they're sometimes better even by the standards of grown-up books. They're not just shorter but also clearer. All the superfluous prose and explanatory side trips have been mercifully swept away.

Yet another great thing about the current crop of middle-grade books your child can now choose from is the impressive number of high-quality graphic novels for this age. Even when children are reading fluently, many still prefer to read visually—books with images that not only support the words but also move the narrative forward. Graphic novels and graphic nonfiction are great ways to keep these kinds of kids hooked on reading. Publishers are on to this—they've added many more graphic novels for middle-grade readers. From realism like Raina Telgemeier's *Smile* or Vera Brosgol's *Be Prepared* to fantasy, like the Dream Jumper books by Greg Grunberg and Lucas Turnbloom, to nonfiction, like the Nathan Hale's Hazardous Tales American history series, older elementary school students and tweens are crazy for these smart, eye-pleasing books. Publishers are also turning successful middle-grade books from years past into graphic novels. Notable ones include Philippa Pearce's classic fantasy *Tom's Midnight Garden*, Lois Lowry's incomparable *The Giver,* and Deborah Ellis's compassionate, eye-opening *The Breadwinner*.

## Here's What You Need to Know

### Let Them Choose Their Own Adventures

This is the time to truly leave your child to his own devices (but not *those* devices). Now that he knows how to read, let him hone in on what he *likes* to read. It's a great time for exploration. Learning which kinds of stories appeal to them and which leave them cold is a process that's best handled on their own. She will be judgmental. She will discard stories you are convinced she will love because she doesn't like the cover. Or because they don't sound "interesting," or because she just plain doesn't want to. And then, she may come around and pick up that same discarded book a year later, especially if you weren't vehement about her reading it.

### Be the Pipeline, Not the Gatekeeper

You want to avoid being too pushy or opinionated, but you are still, after all, the pipeline—the main supplier of books in your child's life. You are probably still the person who takes your kid to the library or brings books home from the library for her. You still buy or borrow or swap books for your child. The trick is to do all of this with an attitude that is on the one hand enthusiastic and on the other hand absolutely nonchalant. So go ahead and plant books around the house that you've tracked down for her. Keep a stack of your own childhood favorites available and just out of the way. The plan is for her to "discover" them herself when she's ready. They will be found, and when they are, they will be opened by your child, and not by you. For many children, it's an important distinction.

### Plant Seeds Where You Can

If your child is open to suggestion, you can be a huge—yet subtle!—influence on your child's reading by suggesting not only your own personal favorites, or books you really think your child will enjoy, but also books you're not even sure she'll like. Kids can really surprise you with their choices. So just casually inform them of what's out there. A child who loves Star Wars may love reading realistic school stories featuring kids just like him, or may be captivated by reading about kids very different from him. She may like sports stories or touching animal stories like *Where the Red Fern Grows*. Think outside his prior reading choices and consider him as a whole person when you make a suggestion. Some kids get overwhelmed by the choices and appreciate suggestions and advice from a trusted adult in their lives.

**Allow for Pure Fun**

Don't be irritatingly ambitious on your child's behalf by pushing litera-ture all the time. Many kids adore joke books, for example, especially when they have an eager listener on hand, ready to fall for it. Find excuses for your child to plunge in. While you're cooking, suggest that your child entertain you with one of her favorite joke books. National Geographic makes some great ones that are heavy on the visuals and kid-friendly humor.

**Reading Outside the Book**

Remember that reading comes in all forms. If your child isn't in a reading phase at the moment, or falls into a feet-dragging mode about books for a while, suggest playing a game instead. Many games heavily incorpo-rate reading, from the obvious candidates like Boggle and Scrabble and Bananagrams to the less obvious ones like games on the Playstation. A number of collectible card games like Magic: The Gathering are text heavy, as are baseball cards. Monopoly has lots of words. All of this is reading.

**Don't Criticize Book Choices — Even Bad Ones**

Don't deny your child a book, even if you think it's terribly written or immature or "beneath her level." Don't weigh in if you notice that the last five books he's read all seem extremely similar. Kids need to decide for themselves what's good and what isn't. And sometimes, a kid just wants to relax with an undemanding diversion, the same way grown-ups do. If, how-ever, your child's gravitation to certain themes, like celebrities, or suicide, concerns you, ask why he finds it interesting. A kid might explain some of what makes him tick when talking about why he likes or is interested in a certain kind of book. That is valuable information for parents of tweens. If the opportunity presents itself, offer your opinion on why certain themes feel superficial or silly or even troubling. But first and foremost, get him talking.

### Keep Reading Aloud

Sure, the teenage years are suddenly in sight, but why give up this mutual pleasure? Besides giving you both the great feeling of sharing a thrilling or funny or heartwarming story with someone you love, it enables you to bring more challenging or emotionally sophisticated books into your rapidly maturing child's world. For instance, if your fourth-grade daughter is dealing with friend drama at school and feeling socially isolated, you could read her *The Hundred Dresses* by Eleanor Estes, a timeless 1945 Newbery Honor book about a Polish girl who wears the same dress every day to school but lies about having one hundered beautiful dresses at home to hide her poverty. That same child might find immeasurable comfort in Shannon Hale's graphic memoir *Real Friends*. Consider paging through it together one evening, reading aloud the dialogue and discussing Shannon's predicament.

### A Community of Readers

One of the great things about contemporary kidlit culture is just how communal it is. Reading was more of a solitary experience before the 1990s. You can thank J. K. Rowling for much of the change. The Harry Potter books ushered in an era in which kids could participate in a lot of excitement around the books they read, from queuing up in stores for a midnight release to visiting an entire theme park that brings fantastical aspects of

the books to life. But it's gone far beyond Harry Potter. Nowadays, children read en masse, and it makes them feel cool to be part of their favorite series' fan group, whether it's Amulet or Divergent or Percy Jackson or the Track series.

### The Wisdom of the Crowd

Communing with other readers is also a great opportunity to motivate kids who may be feeling insecure about their reading ability, and to help them gain confidence. Since it's not in a classroom setting, the point is not how fast you're reading, it's about . . . say, *dragons*. Rather than "What page are you on?" it's "Which dragonet [from Wings of Fire] are you?" The chance to exchange opinions and share enthusiasm with peers can give a reluctant or easily frustrated reader the motivation to keep going.

### Be Open to Unlikely Communities

Reader communities come in all shapes and sizes. If you happen to have a *Minecraft* enthusiast in the household, for example, you may want to check out the huge range of *Minecraft* activity books, guides, novels, and fan fiction. These vehicles offer a new way for *Minecraft* fans to connect with one another when they write and share their own stories, then "like" and comment on others. This is true for Dungeons & Dragons and other popular game-based passions like *Fortnite* as well.

### Authors Can Help

The internet has also made it far easier for children to reach out directly to authors. The kids who used to mail off letters to Beverly Cleary's publisher, never knowing whether they'd be read or responded to, couldn't begin to imagine the wonders available to today's young readers. Many popular writers are on social media or have their own websites, so if your child is on social media or visits those websites, there's a real chance he can reach out to a favorite writer and perhaps even get a direct response. R. J. Palacio, for example, has created a "choosekind" hashtag around the message of *Wonder*. Rick Riordan's Twitter ID is @camphalfblood. (Trust us, this means something to Percy Jackson fans.)

### Fellow Fans Can Help, Too

If your child is especially self-conscious about how he reads, getting him to think beyond the borders of his sibling set, his peer group, or his classroom can really help. There's a whole wide world of readers, and he will quickly find that if he goes onto a message board of kids who like the same books, no one knows how well anyone reads. Moreover, he may have insights into the story line or ideas about the characters that other kids don't have. Now is the time when he realizes that reading isn't just about process but is also about substance, ideas, and discussion. Find legitimate chat rooms by searching publisher and author websites.

### Enthusiasm Is Contagious

Joining communities of readers online can help motivate kids who simply aren't excited about books. If your child sees books as something she "has to" get through, she might find her interest piqued by YouTube videos other kids have made around the books they love. She might find playing a game online based on a book sufficiently entertaining to inspire her to actually pick up the book once iPad time is over. Or you might dangle some online features built around books as a kind of carrot. "Once you've finished the book, let's go online together to check out the website."

### Yes, the Internet Can Encourage Reading

Most children's book publishers have special websites or sections of their websites devoted to popular authors and series where kids can learn more about the books, download extra chapters and bonus features, occasionally play games based on the books or take quizzes on them, and interact with other readers.

## Set Up Shop

Children now create their own kidlit content online, which ranges from reading aloud picture books on YouTube (which can be shared with other online friends or with members of the extended family) to writing their own book reviews to starting their own online fan clubs. So-called "BookTubers" now have thousands of fans following their video reviews. If your child is active online and interested in this, what better way to marry internet life with literary life?

## Get Beyond the "Reading Log" Mentality

Reading logs. What a chore! And what a bore! And also, what a perfect way to invite fudging and white lies ("I read for twenty-three minutes, I swear!"). Maybe worst of all—what a perfect way to turn the joyous and free-form experience of reading into yet another data-generating performance for grown-ups to evaluate. Having to finish up a delicious reading experience with the annoying task of writing it down in a small mandated box can really spoil the pleasure. It's an acknowledged psychological truth that "intrinsic motivation"—having the desire to do something, such as reading, on your own—suffers when the activity is associated with "external controls" such as rewards, punishments, and requirements. But if there's no way around it and your child must keep a reading log as part of her homework, see if you can make the task slightly less odious. You might decide to join him during his mandated twenty minutes of evening reading. Seeing you choose to read can help with your child's attitude, and reading side by side can improve what otherwise might feel like the least helpful kind of homework: "Well, we have a half hour of reading time in our house every night anyway," you might say.

## Consider a Reading Journal Instead

One of the bummers about reading logs is that they are handed in to the teacher on loose-leaf paper or entered into a Google Doc on the class website, where they feel like every other piece of ephemeral homework. They don't belong to the child; they belong to the teacher. But if a child has a special notebook to fill in with the names of the books she's read, it becomes a kind of personal record, and enthusiasm for it grows accordingly. She can illustrate it or decorate it with stickers. It is really *hers*. Whenever she wants to, she can see the accumulated titles she's read, notice a track record in terms of the kinds of books she reads and the challenges she takes on, and look back on it as she gets older, as she would any other diary. This turns a reading log into more of a personal lifelong keepsake than a dreary daily task. You might even consider asking the teacher if your child can have permission to do the required reading log in this way—and who knows, maybe that will inspire a change that benefits all the kids in the class.

## Never Treat Books Like a Chore

Some parents are so eager to get their kids to read, or at least to get off the internet for a few minutes, that they offer incentives to lure their child toward reading material. Don't be tempted! Remember the research on "intrinsic motivation." Rather than saying, "If you spend thirty minutes reading, you'll get to play on the iPad/eat ice cream/be paid a dollar," frame reading as something delightful and special. You might say, "Let's light a fire and snuggle up together with our books" or "Let's pick out which books we want to bring on our trip to Grandma's this weekend" or "I discovered a great bookstore last week—let's go there together and I'll let you pick out two new books." Treat reading as its own reward.

## Guide the Choice

If your child is in a reading rut—choosing the same type of book over and over—and seems open to suggestion, try this "five book choice" system: Choose a couple that veer just slightly off the path—Egyptian myths if he's stuck on the Greeks, for example. Add a couple that bring in some of his nonreading interests, such as camping or baseball, and then one outlier that you're not sure about. Ask him to pick one out of the five that looks most interesting to him, and let him know you're eager to hear what he thinks of it. But also, don't get hung up on the idea of a "rut."

Children benefit from rereading, often gleaning more from the book each time. Rereading is also one of life's sweet pleasures; be grateful she's enjoying herself so much.

### Share Your Childhood Favorite

Let him know more about what you loved to read at his age—how you got into those books, how often you read them, what you loved most, what you remember. (If you still have your childhood copies, show them to him!) You can then slip in what you started reading *after* you were "done" with that series.

### Fostering a Book Critic

Ask your child to "review" a book for you. He can use a five-star system, a thumbs-up/thumbs-down, or a scale from one to ten. The more choice you give him, the more he feels in control of the situation. He's choosing the book; he's choosing the review format. Don't make him write anything down unless he actually really likes writing! Offer to review the book you're reading yourself, too. You can give each other your reviews at the end. He can also go online and write a review on Common Sense Media or another website that encourages kids to post their takes on a book for other prospective readers.

## What to Look For: Middle Grade

### Consider the Age Range

The recommended age range for a middle-grade book is not usually apparent on the book itself. Sometimes you can find it on a publisher's site or in a reputable review. Although the general rule of thumb is that middle-grade books are for ages 8 to 12, that's a pretty big range developmentally, and not every author writes in a way that works for every kid. Many middle-grade books are geared toward either the younger or the older half of the spectrum. If your child is 8 to 10, keep in mind that he may—or may not—be ready for a book with some content that skews older. If your child brings home a book you object to, you will have to decide where you stand on censoring your child's reading choices. Keep in mind that with books—as with movies and TV shows—children can easily tune out or skip over material they're not emotionally ready for. All the risqué content found in PG movies in the 1980s? Much of it washed right over our heads. We find this is especially true with romantic or sexual themes— younger or less emotionally developed kids will sometimes not even notice that stuff is there because they're just not ready to absorb it.

### What's My Place in This Big, Crazy Universe?

Children of this age are interested both in defining their own identities and in investigating questions about the larger world. A good middle-grade book can be surprisingly philosophical, taking on notions like fairness, justice, freedom, and compassion. Some of the best are historical fiction set in challenging time periods like the Civil War, the Holocaust, or the civil rights era. They often deftly address, in an age-appropriate way, real-world problems your child is just becoming aware of: racism, the plight of refugees, the foster-care system, mental illness. Whatever personal challenge your child is navigating—bullying, the end of a friendship, social anxiety, a cross-country move, or death in the family—there is a good middle-grade novel or nonfiction book that can help her get through it. Librarians and experienced booksellers are great resources when you're looking for a book about a particular problem or issue—it's their job, after all, to keep track of what books are out there and match them to the right readers. Ask for a recommendation yourself, or encourage your child to strike up a conversation with one of these friendly experts.

### Kid Versus World

In great middle-grade novels, children are the protagonists; they solve problems, have adventures unmediated by adults, and are generally the stars of

their own shows. That's why orphans are so common in classic children's literature. Even in contemporary middle-grade fiction, parents seem to die or be otherwise unavailable at an improbable rate, forcing young characters to bravely confront challenges. Nonfiction authors, too, have scoured history for stories of children who rose to the occasion and performed heroic acts, whether during the era of slavery or World War II. Others introduce kids to young people who have recently made an impact in other parts of the world, such as Malala Yousafzai, the young Pakistani activist and Nobel Prize winner who stood up for girls' right to an education.

### But Grown-Ups Count, Too

Even so, a great middle-grade book will have at least one admirable adult character, and sometimes a few of them. This is the age at which children realize the grown-up world is fallible, but they still need role models to help and guide them. A sophisticated children's novel can also depict adults behaving badly, or making serious mistakes, and put them into an age-appropriate context.

### Series Are Still Big

Just as with chapter book readers, middle-grade readers like to stay with their favorite characters for multiple books. So keep an eye on the currently popular middle-grade series, whether classics like Lois Lowry's Giver books or newer ones like Soman Chainani's School for Good and Evil books.

### Fantasy Worlds Rule

Many of the best middle-grade books are fantasy, and some of the best fantasy novels, period, were originally intended for middle-grade readers, from *A Wrinkle in Time* to a certain boarding-school wizard. Middle-grade readers like a chance to escape through reading. Fantasy novels offer fully thought-out worlds that have their own rules, with just enough similarity for a young reader to reflect on the rules of his own world. That is to say, they are ideal places to get lost for a child of this age who is ready to challenge boundaries but also, perhaps secretly, is looking for reassurance that the universe is orderly and makes sense.

### Take Home the Gold

The Newbery Medal is in many ways the most prestigious of the awards the American Library Association gives out each year, because it is technically open to any category of book for young readers. The judges' mandate is simply to find "the most distinguished American children's book" of the year. Yet it almost always goes to a middle-grade novel. Same for Newbery Honor books, the runners-up—there are usually anywhere from two to five of these each year, and it's hard to find a dud among the list of past winners. So if you're casting about for a book to bring home to your middle-grade reader and don't feel like doing too much work, it's a good bet a book with that Newbery sticker will turn out to be a winner for your kid, too.

## Be Wary Of

### Know Your Child's Red-Alert Buttons

Some books may be Newbery Honor books, and they may be classics, and they may in fact be terrific books—but they also may be entirely wrong for your child. Some kids just do not like books that feel old-fashioned, or that feature situations they can't relate to, or that have sad endings or characters who die, or . . . fill in the blank.

### Age and Maturity Appropriateness

The label "10 and Up" is often used to show that a particular middle-grade novel may be more sophisticated or that its plot will appeal to older, teenage readers as well. These books may include the more young-adult-appealing themes of loss, drugs, sex, and gray areas of friendship. There is a big difference between a young 8-year-old and a world-weary, teenagery 12-year-old, and the middle-grade literature that falls on the older end of that age range might not interest your younger child in the least—or might be needlessly upsetting. A mature 10- or 11-year-old might be eager to dip into *The Hunger Games*, but it's something quite different for that sensitive 9-year-old. Again, when in doubt, find a reliable review to check if it's right for your child, given his age and maturity level.

# Our Middle-Grade Novel Picks

### When You Reach Me
**Rebecca Stead**
In this taut novel about a girl who receives notes that seem to be coming from someone who knows the future, every word, every sentence has meaning and substance.

### The Watsons Go to Birmingham—1963
**Christopher Paul Curtis**
A shy 9-year-old African American boy heads with his big, loving family from Flint, Michigan, down to Alabama to visit his grandmother. Curtis knows how to propel a story forward while keeping it both comic and deeply moving.

### The One and Only Ivan
**Katherine Applegate**
Nearly all kids appreciate a great animal story. Inspired by the true story of a captive gorilla known as Ivan, this illustrated book is told from the point of view of Ivan himself.

### Matilda AND Danny the Champion of the World
**Roald Dahl**
We are split on which of these two Dahl classics is most unmissable. The point is, Dahl's novels still deliver a great deal to young readers, so work in as many as you can.

### Brown Girl Dreaming
**Jacqueline Woodson**

This memoir-in-verse, perfect for readers ages 10 and up, sweeps personal and African American history into one lyrical, flowing story of one girl's experience of growth, change, and family and community bonds. Praised by critics, teachers, and readers, it won the National Book Award, a Newbery Honor, and a stamp of approval from Barack Obama and Oprah Winfrey when it was published in 2014.

### Mrs. Frisby and the Rats of NIMH
**Robert C. O'Brien**
In this Newbery Medal–winning classic, a widowed mouse mother of four faces a terrible dilemma, one that can be solved only with the assistance of genetically modified, super-intelligent rats.

### The Phantom Tollbooth
**Norton Juster,**
**illustrated by Jules Feiffer**
This remarkable, original book stands the test of time (and why shouldn't it, with a watchdog named Tock?). Full of wordplay and thought puzzles, it will tempt grown-ups to reread it themselves.

### The Girl Who Drank the Moon
**Kelly Barnhill**

A kind witch bestows the power of magic on a little baby in this Newbery Medalist, a timeless, plot-twisty, politically aware, and truly enchanting tale.

### Tuck Everlasting
**Natalie Babbitt**

If you could live forever, would you? This novel about a family that stumbles on a fountain of youth offers a nuanced exploration of that eternal philosophical question. You finish it with a new understanding of mortality and of yourself.

### From the Mixed-Up Files of Mrs. Basil E. Frankweiler
**E. L. Konigsburg**

More than fifty years after this book first appeared, it's still impossible not to be dazzled by Claudia Kincaid, the heroine who runs away from the suburbs with her younger brother to the Metropolitan Museum of Art, outwitting adults left and right and following her own brilliant, kooky ideas of freedom and bliss.

## Our Middle-Grade Series Picks

### Birchbark House
**Louise Erdrich**

The story of a young Ojibwa girl living on an island in Lake Superior around 1847, this series by the acclaimed adult author Erdrich forms a kind of counterpart to the Little House books by Laura Ingalls Wilder—the same history of white expansion into the West, told from the Native American perspective.

### The Melendy quartet
**Elizabeth Enright**

A novelist who wrote for *The New Yorker* tells about a family of largely self-parented kids making their way in New York in the 1940s. The quartet includes *The Saturdays* and *The Four-Story Mistake*. We also recommend her stand-alone novel, *Gone-Away Lake*.

### Loki's Wolves trilogy
**K. L. Armstrong and Melissa Marr**

Including *Odin's Ravens* and *Thor's Serpents*, this mythology-infused adventure trilogy takes place in the Black Hills of South Dakota.

### Percy Jackson
**Rick Riordan**

A boy battles mythological monsters in this action-packed, wildly popular series. Actually, there are three separate series set within the Percy Jackson universe, developed by a former teacher with "reluctant" boy readers in mind. The hero's strength derives from his dyslexia, and the rest of the cast is notably diverse.

## The Wayside School series
### Louis Sachar

By now a couple of generations of kids have been captivated by Sachar's zany, brainy stories about a school fifty stories high but with no nineteenth  floor. There's math and wordplay galore, making the whole concept of school into something like a game.

## The Grimm trilogy
### Adam Gidwitz

Hansel and Gretel and Jack and Jill as you never knew them: taking back their destinies and righting the wrongs of traditional fairy tales. It has all the gore and chills of Grimm but subversive laughs and empowerment, too.

## How to Train Your Dragon
### Cressida Cowell

A gentle boy named Hiccup must catch and train a dragon to be initiated into a Viking clan. These clever tales are heroic and silly all at once. The movies are fine, too, though with Cowell's revved-up drawings, the pages leap to life all on their own.

## A Series of Unfortunate Events
### Lemony Snicket

This tragicomic saga of three orphans stuck with an uncle who's trying to steal their inheritance has the dark humor certain kids thrive on. These books' self-conscious narrator has spawned many imitators, but Snicket (real name: Daniel Handler) is a true original.

## The Track series
### Jason Reynolds

Each member of the Defenders track team has a particular competitive strength as well as a distinct personality and voice. Each narrates one of these books, in which their challenges can be even bigger off the track than on it.

## The Geniuses series
### Michael Dante DiMartino

This action-adventure series takes place in a Renaissance-inspired world, with all the imaginative world building you'd expect from one of the creators of the  anime TV (and accompanying graphic novel) show *Avatar: The Last Airbender*.

# Our Post-Harry-Potter-Slump Picks

Y our child has read Harry Potter, and now nothing seems quite as good. But there is a lot of life beyond Harry!

### The Oz books
**L. Frank Baum**

Everyone knows the *Wonderful Wizard of Oz* story, but mostly through the movie rather than the book. One of the great appeals of the Oz books for Potter fans is that Baum created a fully realized world and carried it through a series of long books.

### The Animorphs series
**K. A. Applegate**

This series, written by the Newbery Medalist Katherine Applegate, is easier going than the Harry Potter books and less literary. But the books create an engaging fantasy world for readers in which kids transform into various creatures. Bonus: There are lots of books in the series. Applegate's newer, environmentally conscious fantasy series, The Endlings, is also great.

### The Warriors series AND The Survivors series
**Erin Hunter**

These series take place in worlds in which cats and dogs (respectively) rule. Children who get into these books tend to *really* get into them. There are several volumes as well as subseries of six books each. It can feel like an endless number of titles to parents, but not to the books' fans. FYI, *Erin Hunter* is a pseudonym for five prolific and accomplished children's-books writers who work as a team.

### The Nevermoor books
**Jessica Townsend**

A cursed girl born on an unlucky day. A secret magical city called Nevermoor. A world full of magic and peril. Yes, it's Harry Potteresque, and it's also very good.

### The Mysterious Benedict Society series
**Trenton Lee Stewart**

An orphan boy takes a strange test and gains admittance to the prestigious Learning Institute for the Very Enlightened. Naturally, all is not as it seems. Clever, quirky, and thoroughly engaging.

### The Lockwood and Co. series
**Jonathan Stroud**

A small, child-run detective agency in London investigates problems of a ghostly nature. Suspenseful and smart, with heavy doses of deadpan humor.

### The Unwanteds series
**Lisa McMann**
In this dystopian series, all 13-year-olds are labeled Wanted, Necessary, or Unwanted, putting a set of twin boys into separate categories. Suspense and adventure follow. There's also a spinoff series, Unwanteds Quests.

### Miss Peregrine's Peculiar Children series
**Ransom Riggs**
Original both in terms of story and format (vintage photographs appear throughout), the story of 16-year-old Jacob and the boarding school for "peculiar"

children he discovers is at once creepy, twisted, fantastical, and stirring, about adolescence and about all ages. For older Harry Potter fans.

### The Five Elements series
**Dan Jolley**
Four friends must save San Francisco from imminent destruction. This magical adventure series also contains plenty of humor to leaven the peril.

### The Darkest Minds series
**Alexandra Bracken**
After being sent by her parents for mysterious reasons to a government-run rehabilitation facility at age 10, Ruby escapes at 16. But what's happened to the rest of the world's children, and why? A creepy and dark dystopic adventure for older tweens and teens.

# What to Look For:
# Middle-Grade Graphic Novels

## Story and Style Count

Although graphic-format books tend to be crowd pleasers, they are not all built alike. Just as your child will have preferences in non-graphic-format books, she will also care about the kinds of graphic books she spends time with. For example, a kid who gravitates toward action and adventure in a novel is going to appreciate that genre in graphic novel format as well.

## Consider an Adaptation

From *Black Beauty* to *Coraline* to *Artemis Fowl*, many classics and recent popular children's titles are being reimagined as graphic novels. If your child liked the original, she might also enjoy reading a graphic version—

and perhaps it will excite her even more. And even if it doesn't make her top-ten list, she might find it interesting to compare the two forms of storytelling.

### Don't Shy Away from the Serious

Some of the best graphic novels and memoirs for adults have taken on very serious subjects, from the Holocaust (*Maus*) to parental death (*Can't We Talk About Something More Pleasant?*). Similarly, for children, graphic formats have tackled subjects like refugees, discrimination, and gender identity. For some kids, encountering these topics in a graphic format might prove easier to handle.

# Be Wary Of

### Grown-Up Fare

Most kids' novels and nonfiction books look obviously like they're for younger readers, and ditto for adult books—but this is not always true for graphic novels. Some adult graphic novels may at first glance look like they're meant for younger readers. Smaller publishers, especially, might not bother to differentiate the look of their graphic novels for the age of their intended audience, so check them out closely before you bring them home.

### Too Much of a Good Thing

It's possible to, at times, get so excited about the appeal of graphic novels that you push a few too many on your children—at the expense of the words-only books that can also mean so much to a middle-grade reader. As important as recognizing and facilitating visual reading is, don't let graphic novels completely replace books constructed entirely of words.

# Our Middle-Grade Graphic Novel Picks

### Roller Girl
**Victoria Jamieson**
Astrid joins a roller-derby camp before she begins junior high, but can she keep up with the older girls and stay close to her dance-crazy best friend? Jamieson is great at capturing the emotions of a kid who feels like an outsider and the small changes that add up to big passages in a young life.

### Zita the Spacegirl
**Ben Hatke**
Zita's best friend, Joseph, is abducted by aliens, so she zooms into space to rescue him, encountering crazy creatures and outwitting intergalactic monsters. Hatke's *Mighty Jack*, a modernized "Jack and the Beanstalk" tale, is equally appealing. His smoothly balanced art and storytelling never fail to draw you in.

### Giants Beware!
**Jorge Aguirre,**
**illustrated by Rafael Rosado**
This trilogy (the others are *Dragons Beware!* and *Monsters Beware!*) features a feisty heroine and slayer of beasts named Claudette, whose adventures are distinguished by ample humor, richly colored drawings, and plenty of updated fairy tale–flavored adventure.

### My Neighbor Totoro Picture Book
**Hayao Miyazaki**
The companion graphic novel version of the beloved anime classic is a wonderful way to introduce or enrich a child's movie experience, but it also stands on its own as a rich and complex story of friendship.

### Fairy Tale Comics, Fable Comics, AND Nursery Rhyme Comics
**Multiple authors,**
**published by First Second Books**
Fairy tales, plus comics: Need we say more? Ditto fables and nursery rhymes. Kids love meeting familiar tales in a vividly visual format.

### Nimona
**Noelle Stevenson**
Based on a popular webcomic, this stellar graphic novel for ages 10 and up turns the superhero plot on its head, with a young female shapeshifter who signs on as official sidekick to a villain trying to rehabilitate his image.

### My Beijing: Four Stories of Everyday Wonder
**Nie Jun**
These wonderful connected stories— with a sprinkling of time travel—feature a girl with a disability that limits her walking but doesn't hold her back from exploring her lively neighborhood. The vibe calls to mind a Miyazaki movie, but sweeter.

### Sunny Side Up
**Jennifer L. Holm and Matthew Holm**
It's the 1970s, and 10-year-old Sunny is sent to spend the summer with her dotty but well-meaning grandfather in

Florida because her parents are dealing with her teenage brother's problems, which, she learns later, involve drugs. Funny, realistic, and an important look at family addiction from a younger sibling's point of view. And there's an equally good follow-up, *Swing It, Sunny*.

### Be Prepared
**Vera Brosgol**
A funny, uplifting summer-camp tale with a twist: Vera is a 12-year-old Russian immigrant trying, and failing, to fit in with the American girls. A summer camp in upstate New York for Russian-speaking kids seems like the answer, but a whole new set of challenges awaits, starting with the latrines.

### New Kid
**Jerry Craft**
Jordan, an African American boy, goes to an elite, mostly white prep school in this funny, nuanced book about race, class, and navigating differences. Craft makes Jordan a gifted artist and blends in his razor-sharp tween's-eye drawings seamlessly.

# Our Picks:
# Graphic Memoirs and Nonfiction

### Nathan Hale's Hazardous Tales
Each tale, supposedly authored by the Revolutionary War hero Nathan Hale on the eve of his execution by the British, presents a dramatic episode in American history. These are solidly factual yet cinematic, character-filled, and stirring.

### Smile
**Raina Telgemeier**
Raina experiences braces, boy troubles, and other plagues of the sixth grade in the first of these insightful, uplifting favorites from the emotionally astute Telgemeier. After this one, it's pretty much a given that elementary school readers head straight for her *Drama* and *Sisters*.

### El Deafo
**Cece Bell**
In this touching and astute memoir of going to school with hearing loss, author Bell draws herself as a long-eared bunny and transforms her disability into a superpower.

### Real Friends
**Shannon Hale**
A very outgoing but socially blundering girl narrates this funny, realistic story from Hale's own childhood. Charming, and a lifesaver for kids with social challenges getting their first taste of "friend drama."

### To Dance
**Siena Cherson Siegel,
illustrated by Mark Siegel**
The rigor, beauty, and heartbreak of
a young ballerina's life is told with
elegance and a touch of melancholy.
You'll also learn a lot about ballet.

### The Faithful Spy:
### Dietrich Bonhoeffer and
### the Plot to Kill Hitler
**John Hendrix**
Kids are fascinated by World War II, and
this story of the Christian minister who
organized against Hitler and even plotted an assassination attempt is action
packed and morally complex. Be ready
for some deep, important conversations
about what good people can do when
they see evil.

### Human Body Theater
**Maris Wicks**
A trip through the human body,
presented as a theatrical spectacular.
You'll be surprised at how well kids
can understand scientific concepts
when they're presented this clearly
and entertainingly.

### Women in Science
**Rachel Ignotofsky**
Okay, it's not technically a
graphic novel, but this bestselling
compendium of mini-biographies
of female science greats works
facts and life stories into graphically
interesting illustrations with maximum
visual appeal. Each page is worth
lingering over.

## Our Graphic Novel Series Picks

### Hilda and the Bird Parade AND
### RELATED Hilda stories
**Luke Pearson**
An intrepid blue-haired girl must make
her own way in a mysterious and
magical world that intersects with the
real world of an atmospheric, vaguely
European city.

### The Bone series
**Jeff Smith**
The great Bone saga is credited with
kicking off the graphic novel boom for
kids. The central characters are bones
(trust us) called Fone Bone, Phoney
Bone, and Smiley Bone, who meet new
friends, and some scary monsters, when
they're forced to venture into a valley
outside of Boneville.

### The Crafty Cat series
**Charise Mericle Harper**
Yes, there are sweet and adorable graphic novels featuring second-grade girls, school preparedness, and handicrafts. This one doubles as a great early reader.

### The Nnewts series
**Doug TenNapel**
It's amphibians versus reptiles in this richly imagined world, in which our tiny hero must outwit mutant lizards to avenge his home and family.

### The Last Kids on Earth series
**Max Brallier,**
**illustrated by Douglas Holgate**
Zombies! Lots of them, and 13-year-old Jack, an abandoned foster child, must fight for survival. Like many great zombie tales, this one is also very funny.

### The Dog Man series
**Dav Pilkey**
This series, for slightly older children than Pilkey's Captain Underpants series, has less potty humor and is surprisingly emotionally astute. It is also as hilarious as his more famous series. Maybe more so.

### The Treehouse series
**Andy Griffiths,**
**illustrated by Terry Denton**
Rife with hyperbole, crass humor, and over-the-top boy behavior, these books are an international sensation for good reason. Any Wimpy Kid fan will love them.

### The Dream Jumper series
**Greg Grunberg,**
**illustrated by Lucas Turnbloom**
Ben can jump into other people's dreams, which comes into use when his friends fall prey to a nightmarish monster. It's nice to see stories about boys helping their friends.

### The Olympians series
**George O'Connor**
Superhero comics–style retellings of the Greek myths, god by goddess by demigod. What's not to like about that?

### The Amulet series
**Kazu Kibuishi**
Not for the young or easily frightened, this dark and atmospheric series follows a brother and sister who, in the wake of their father's death, seek to rescue their kidnapped mother. There are monsters.

# What to Look For:
# Middle-Grade Audiobooks

### All Ears

Audiobooks, particularly on car rides, make it easy for children and adults of different ages to participate in the enjoyment of a shared story. Certain classic and contemporary favorites, such as *Stuart Little* or *Harry Potter and the Chamber of Secrets* or any Percy Jackson book, can sweep aside the occasional protests of suddenly snooty older tween and teen listeners ("I remember this!" "I used to love this book!"), all the while raising the bar for younger readers, who will be rapt by what their older siblings like. At the very least, these audiobooks will hit a massive sweet spot for one child in the car while pleasantly diverting everyone else.

### Captive Audience

Take advantage of the fact that when you're in the car traveling with kids, they have nowhere else to go. It allows you the chance to expose your kids to something they might otherwise resist, whether it's a collection of Greek myths or Norwegian folktales. And if one child simply refuses to participate, she can always pop in a pair of earbuds and listen to her own story while the rest of the group enjoys what's playing through the car speakers.

### Solo Listening

Many children have access to a digital device with earbuds and already listen to music and podcasts on their own. Why not let them add audiobooks to the mix? Many books on audio are low-cost, and you might even consider allowing her to get her own subscription (or access to a family subscription) through a digital audiobook service like Audible. This will give her the freedom to choose what she listens to and allow her the choice of immersing herself in books just as she does with her favorite music, whether she's walking to school, going for a run, or sitting in the backseat of a car.

### Free — or Close to It

Most libraries have great collections of audio discs as well as download-able options. Also, many great stories are in the public domain and can be downloaded for free or low cost online. With little to no financial investment, you can easily start a story and abandon it halfway through if it doesn't suit your tastes.

### From the Horse's Mouth

Not every author excels at reading out loud, so if a publisher has made the author of the book the narrator, it's because he's good at it. Who better to hear from than the person who wrote the book? The author knows exactly what the evil troll sounds like.

### Star Power — or Not

Some actors are brilliant at reading audiobooks: Emma Thompson, Stephen Fry, Kate Winslet, and Jim Dale are among them. Other stars are far better suited to the screen. Rather than immediately select a reading from a favorite actor, listen to a snippet online before you buy a disc or download.

### Re-"reads"

As readers, we all have the occasional craving to revisit a world we've loved — it's like checking back in with an old friend — and audio is an especially great way to enjoy a story for a second or a sixtieth time. Kids get a lot out of reconsidering books even two or three years after they first read them, because they've inevitably changed a lot in that time and can note how their reactions are different this time. And it's an easy lift — any 11-year-old who spaces out listening to *Harry Potter and the Order of the Phoenix* will easily be able to resume wherever he checks back in.

# Be Wary Of

### Gratuitous Sound Effects

Sometimes, sounds can be employed to useful effect, but other times, it's just a whole lot of noise. Dr. Seuss does not need a lot of bells and whistles with the right narration. If you can, listen to a snippet online first.

### Unwanted Abridgments

Most kids want the full story. Of course, in certain cases, really long books or classic tales for all ages are better in abridged formats, depending on the audience. The fact that it's abridged should be on the front, but read the fine print front and back to be sure you're not getting a shorter version by accident.

### Too Many Characters

Wait, who are we talking about again? Is this the villain or the hero's grandfather? Unfamiliar stories with lots of characters can be hard to track on audio—even more so than in a book—because it's not as easy to rewind to a precise spot the way you can reread the last paragraph in a book.

# Our Audiobook Picks for Families

**Charlotte's Web**
**E. B. White,**
**narrated by E. B. White**
This may be the best audiobook of all time for the entire family. White's East Coast drawl seems to hardly exist anymore—and it's the perfect vehicle for this story. His telling is devoid of silliness or sentimentality. And if you don't get moist-eyed hearing his soft "goodbyes" as each baby spider takes flight near the end, you're made of sterner stuff than we are.

**Harry Potter**
**J. K. Rowling,**
**narrated by Jim Dale or Stephen Fry**
Fights have broken out over which audio version is better, the American Dale or the British Fry. Let's settle it now: They

are both great. Enjoy one or the other or alternate both and let your children compare.

### My Father's Dragon, Elmer and the Dragon, AND The Dragons of Blueland

**Ruth Stiles Gannett, narrated by Robert Sevra**

These classic adventure stories still work as well as they did when the first one came out in 1948, winning a Newbery Honor, and Sevra's narration is smooth and soothing, making this book work equally well for kids as young as 5 and as old as 12.

### The Roald Dahl Audio Collection

**Roald Dahl, narrated by Roald Dahl**

Even if you're already a die-hard Roald Dahl fan in print, you'll appreciate him all the more when you hear him read his own stories. There are many versions of his books on audio, but none are as wonderful as Dahl reading from The Roald Dahl Audio Collection. One caveat: The stories are sadly abridged in these versions. They are worth it anyway for the narrator, who reels off his gleefully nasty character descriptions and caustic dialogue in his distinctive Nordic-inflected British accent.

### Tales from the Odyssey

**Mary Pope Osborne, narrated by James Simmons**

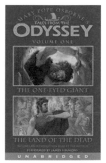

For some young readers, there is simply never enough Greek mythology. Why not bring the gods into yet another format? This simplified audio version of Homer's tale is a fine introduction for young children and tweens interested in Greek gods and heroes, and a gift for adults keen to brush up—painlessly—on the ancient masterpiece.

# PART FOUR

# A Reader for Life: Teenagers

# YOUR TEEN READER

Three confident steps forward, one stumbling, ankle-spraining step back . . . Being the parent of a teenager can be head spinning and heart wrenching—not since toddlerhood has your child undergone so much developmental change in so short a time. Despite the bad rap adolescence so often gets, there are joys, even thrills, as you watch your child edge closer and closer to the independent person he or she is becoming—especially when it comes to reading. In fact, what's ahead now may come as a pleasant surprise. Since you went through those same tumultuous teenage years, a new, energized culture of books meant specifically for teenagers has developed.

"Young adult literature" is a category that didn't even exist a few decades ago, but these days it is loud and proud. YA books now take up a hefty share of space in bookstores and libraries. Their authors are rock stars: We've been blown away by the sight of long, snaking lines of teenagers waiting patiently to get their books signed at appearances by authors like Gayle Forman, Angie Thomas, John Green, and Jenny Han. Books by these same authors become hit movies with a startling frequency. (See *If I Stay, The Hate U Give, The Fault in Our Stars, To All the Boys I've Loved Before*.) Festivals devoted entirely to books for and about teenagers are hot tickets across the country, from South Carolina's YALLFest to Santa Monica's YALLWest. And here's an open secret in the books world: Many YA readers are actually over 21. These books are not just throwaway teenage pleasures; many of them are well-written, sensitive, nuanced pieces of literature for readers of all ages. They're just created especially with adolescents in mind.

Many lifelong readers remember adolescence as a time of intense immersion in books, a period in which you read to help figure out who you were, what you believed in, and where you stood in the world. Literature can provide role models and heroes and antiheroes. Books can impart truths about how the world operates, both in real terms and through ideals. A made-up story or the biography of someone important can offer a path to take or one to avoid. In short, the teenage years are a great time to learn to channel frustration, sorrow, confusion, and loneliness through literature—and to find solace and company and hope for the future in books.

But where, exactly, do parents come into all that? If you're wise, you're not barreling in through the front door of your teenager's reading life. Parenting adolescents, after all, is about strategically stepping back so they can find their own way. But you still play a role—an important one. Sometimes it involves helping your kid find books he'll like. Sometimes it involves figuring out why she has *stopped* reading or never seemed to read as much as you'd (or she'd) have liked. Whatever the case in your family, your job now is to get to know as well as you can the passions and preferences of your own ever-evolving, independence-seeking teenager, and the landscape of books that are out there to help her, tempt her, console her, and inspire her.

## Here's What You Need to Know

### A Little YA History

Contemporary middle-grade novels tend to have main characters around 11 years old, sometimes 12. But even though these novels are marketed as being for 8- to 12-year-olds, we know that kids like, and often prefer, to read about kids slightly older than themselves. That means a lot of 11- and 12-year-olds start to lose interest in these middle-grade books and begin peering down the road into the realm of young adult literature. But how do you know when they're ready for it?

That's a tough question to answer, not only because every kid is different, but also because as the category of "young adult" books has grown and evolved, it has inevitably expanded—so much so that at times it can be hard to say exactly what makes a book YA in the first place and not, say, an adult novel or a fantasy series that just happens to have a teenage protagonist. Remember, YA is relatively new: Just a generation ago, teenagers got by with snagging romances by Danielle Steel and potboilers by Sidney Sheldon off their parents' shelves, or passing around the incest melodramas of V. C. Andrews or Judy Blume's distinctly adult book, *Wifey*, among friends, feeling like they were in on something top secret and transgressive.

### What Makes a Book "YA"?

A good rule of thumb is that a book *for* adults but *about* a teenager will be *looking back* on the experience of adolescence with grown-up eyes, giving plenty of reference points adults will relate to. A YA book, in contrast, plunges the reader directly into the experience of being a teenager—that confusing, exhilarating, hormone-fueled, high-stakes time when you really don't know what the future will hold for you or what adulthood is actually like. You aren't reflecting on adolescence; you are full-throttle immersed in it. A YA book can have well-developed adult characters, but they are not the ones whose fate is on the line; they are often the "other"—the authority, the voice of reason, the enemy, the solace. In all things, the teenage perspective dominates, as characters experience the bliss and terror of many important firsts: first love, first time away from home, first encounter with some brutal realities of the social and political world.

### Growing Older Younger

Today's YA has come so far that it has its own genres and subgenres, from gritty novels in verse by writers like Ellen Hopkins to graphic novels by Mariko and Jillian Tamaki to futuristic thrillers by writers like Marie Lu. These books have arrived at a time when we're witnessing the trend of *growing older younger*, in which kids seem to do all kinds of things at age 11 that formerly didn't occur until age 14. So kids who have tired of middle-grade books now have a banquet of literary possibilities spread out before them. We all know many elementary school–age children, for example, who've already worked their way through the later YA-oriented volumes of Harry Potter, which include the distressing death of a high school student. You are not the only parent who wonders whether this is for the best.

Young adult books—with their edgy dialogue, occasionally troubling adolescent behavior, violence, sexuality, and political themes—are an adjustment for many parents, especially when your children aren't yet teenagers. Alas, adolescence often begins with an attitude shift that predates an actual plunge into full-on puberty, which itself is beginning at ever younger ages, especially for girls, who can begin to exhibit hormonal shifts as young as age 8. Whether or not your tween is emotionally able to process young adult lit, she may very well want to plunge into it—and at a much younger age than you expected.

### Rebellion Is Still the Norm

If you remember anything about your own pre-teen and teenage behavior, you may remember one word: *rebellion*. At the moment, you may feel utterly alarmed at the thought of your 11-year-old reading *The Hunger Games*, that contemporary classic by Suzanne Collins about a dystopic future in which a malevolent ruling class stages tournaments where children and teenagers must fight each other to the death. But bear in mind that the purpose the book is serving for your child may be largely symbolic. She may want to read the book because it will make her feel—or seem—"tough," "advanced," or "in the know." For one thing, the fact that she wants to signal to the world those things about herself *by reading a book* should be reassuring. And there can be a safety in reading about transgressive acts; you're not *doing* any of these things yourself—you're just reading about them and figuring them out. You are learning to make judgments and to draw your own conclusions.

### Where the Opportunities Lie

Watching your child gravitate to a book you are just not sure about is a complicated moment. In a way, the predicament captures a lot about parenthood in general: It's exciting (my kid's reading!), overwhelming (my kid's reading *that*?), and filled with opportunity, all at once. As far as disturbing content goes—say, that small matter of child-on-child killing—think of it as, first of all, a chance to have a deep conversation. Ask lots of questions. As you try to decide whether you're okay with her reading a certain book, be sure to discuss your own feelings as frankly as possible. For *The Hunger Games*, you might say, "In this book, children are forced to kill other children, and I find that really disturbing. I'm afraid reading about that will scare you or make you think dark thoughts about the world." You may be surprised by the sophistication of her response, and you'll almost definitely be rewarded by the chance to have a substantive conversation about how the culture she's exposed to affects her—and what a book can mean in her life. Also, know this: *The Hunger Games*, although violent, has a lot of heart, beginning with a teenager's sacrifice for her younger sister and mother. Collins has said she intended the book to be an antiwar novel, above all, and we think it performs that role powerfully. These are tough lessons to learn, but YA authors (and their publishers) take their responsibility to properly contextualize these issues very seriously. Children can learn about difficult subjects in many ways—online, through friends, in the schoolyard, by overhearing conversations on a city bus. Here, in books, they are learning those lessons in what may well be the best conceivable environment.

### Let Them Read Alone

Teenagers seek comfort, celebration, and empathy through stories, whether they're told via social media, a movie, or a book. Adolescence is typically a pretty egotistical and dramatic time of life. For kids who feel simultaneously all alone (Nobody could possibly understand me!) and desperate to belong (Why doesn't anybody understand me?), literature can provide powerful company. Kids are looking to find themselves and like-minded people through the books they read, just as they do in real life, on social media, and in the hallways at school. If your teenager holes up with a book and doesn't want to talk about it, don't fret. She may not want to discuss a book that deals with menstrual pain, cutting, depression, or vampire sex with their parents, and that's okay. (Sometimes, teenagers are in fact worried that you'll worry about them! Their response may well be "Don't freak out, Mom. I'm not going to become bulimic; I'm just reading about it.")

### Send Them Online

You read that right. For one thing, YA authors usually have a strong social media presence, which they use to communicate with their fans in real time. It's a great way to keep teenagers talking and thinking about books, even when they're on the internet. Authors like Tahereh Mafi, Brendan Kiely, Dhonielle Clayton, and Sarah Dessen are great at the social media game, using it to share stories about their lives, joke around with one another, recommend books, weigh in on current events, and just generally act as a welcoming, encouraging presence for teenage readers. They often reply directly to fans, and they occasionally stage spontaneous contests for book giveaways or participate in impromptu live chats. So if your teenager likes a book, make sure he knows that the author is very likely on Twitter, Instagram, and Facebook.

YA blogs are also a way to stay up to date with the steady stream of new books appearing every month. Book Riot, The YA Bookshelf, Girl Plus Book, and similar sites update their book lists regularly—they can be a good resource when your teenager is searching for a particular genre or type of story, or just wants to know what's new and popular out there.

### Remember Movie Night

There are many book-to-movie hits for the YA crowd. Although you may not be super excited about watching *Divergent* unfold cinematically, your 13-year-old daughter will probably be riveted. At least the social hierarchies of her middle school aren't *that* cruel! Give her the Veronica Roth trilogy to read, and when she's finished, watch the movie together. Or maybe you have an older teenager who's just discovering Rick Yancey's 5th Wave series about alien attacks. You can cap off that experience with a viewing of the movie starring Chloë Grace Moretz and Tobey Maguire, safe in the confines of your home.

### Stop and Shop

If you're running errands with your teenager, include a visit to the local bookstore. It's a bit of a sneak attack, but the idea is to create opportunities to integrate books into his life whenever you can. He may get encouraged or excited to read something if forced to roam the aisles on his own while you browse. And of course, casually offer to buy him anything that seems especially alluring. Or, if that's not in the budget, look for books that you can later find at the library.

### Let Them Download

If you can swing it financially, offer to pay for any books your teenager downloads on Audible or iTunes, and set him up with the downloadable app connected to the local library. Connect your phone to the car's speakers and listen to the book together when you road trip or drive him to school. This has the added benefit of bringing you into his stories (even if it's not the particular story you'd have chosen for yourself or for him). You may find your sulky teenager actually *sharing* his thoughts about what you're both listening to.

### Join the Club

Mother-daughter book clubs have become a nationwide trend, and we're sure there are father-son clubs, too. Why not one that includes grandparents, for that matter? In fact, asking your parents or in-laws to read a book with your teenager can provide a rich bonding experience. Kids may

## Is It Ever Too Late?

One of the most surprising things people hear from a successful writer is "I don't remember reading much when I was younger." We've heard it more often than you'd think—and their confessions contain great inspiration and reassurance for the parents of teenagers who don't seem to take an interest in books.

Take the bestselling author Matt de la Peña, who has written for children of all age levels, including teenagers. His picture book *Last Stop on Market Street*, illustrated by Christian Robinson, won the 2016 Newbery Medal, which very rarely goes to a picture book. This powerhouse of children's storytelling speaks often about his teenage years, when he played basketball nonstop and never voluntarily cracked a book. He remembers that he did not even think of reading fiction or a full-on book of any kind. When he had to spend time in the school library, he'd flip through sports magazines. Looking back now, he says, he realizes that he was actually trawling those articles about athletes for stories about *life*. Where did the players come from, what were their families like, how did they manage to get to the big leagues? Who helped them or didn't help them? Those pieces of information—those story arcs— riveted him more than the statistics or analyses did.

He got to college on a basketball scholarship and in an English class was assigned a novel that changed his life: *The House on Mango Street* by Sandra Cisneros. There he saw something about his own life and his own family, and that thrilled him. He began reading more fiction and never stopped. Soon enough he started writing. You never would have thought that would be the direction his life would take if you'd known him when he was a teenager, obsessed with basketball and completely indifferent to any form of writing that didn't concern sports. But what he was really looking for were stories about people like himself.

One lesson to take from de la Peña's story is that it's important to think about all the kinds of reading your teenager does, and acknowledge all of it *as reading*. The comics he still keeps up with, the website that collects humorous memes that she checks every day—these are signs that your teenager is a reader, even if full-length novels are not in the picture right now. Is there a way to find books that somehow dovetail with those inter- ests or the particular quest he seems to be on at the moment? Maybe his favorite YouTuber has written a book (a strangely large proportion of them do). An actor's or sports star's memoir might be the ticket, or a funny book about the female experience that you hear your nieces loved, like Amy Schumer's *The Girl with the Lower Back Tattoo*. Just as de la Peña was moved by the familiar heritage in Cisneros's book, be aware of those books in which your teen may see a reflection of her life and experiences. You may think she is bent on rebelling and rejecting everything about her family, but the reality is that she is searching for affirmation of herself—her past, present, and future. A book is an ideal place to find that.

be especially interested in joining a multigenerational book club if their friends are in it, too, so team up with your kid's friends' parents to see if you can build the kind of club yours would enjoy. Conversely, some kids may be especially interested if the club includes some of *your* friends, too; they like seeing their parents in a less buttoned-up role, relaxing with their own friends rather than always playing "the parent." And there's nothing like getting a group of readers together for generating book recommendations, naturally and easily. If your daughter witnesses a friend's especially "cool" mom enjoying a book, she may be motivated to appreciate it as well, or to enthuse over a book she sees other kids she admires enjoy.

## On a Mission

Teenagers like reading about the things that matter most to them, and about their place in the world, which today means a surge in books—both novels and nonfiction, realism and fantasy—that address issues like social justice, sexual harassment, gun violence, gender identity, racial and religious prejudice, immigration, poverty, and the environment. These books put difficult subjects into an age-appropriate context and deal with them in a thoughtful, productive way. What's more, the authors increasingly see addressing these issues through the books they write as a kind of mission. Well-written, sensitive, empowering books are emerging from this cultural change; Angie Thomas's bestselling *The Hate U Give* has been followed by other novels about police killings of unarmed black teenagers, including Jay Coles's *Tyler Johnson Was Here* and Mark Oshiro's *Anger Is a Gift*. Whether a book is set in today's world, on a distant planet, or two hundred years in the future, stories of authoritarian governments, social oppression, and environmental devastation resonate strongly with teenagers taking their first long, hard look at the world around them. In fact, many observers have noted that the rise in teenage political activism, such as the #NeverAgain campaign against gun violence started by the students at Marjory Stoneman Douglas High School in Parkland, Florida, after the mass shooting there in 2018, calls to mind bestselling fantasy books like Victoria Aveyard's Red Queen series, in which articulate, impassioned teenagers are forced to fight back and speak out against an adult political establishment that they think treats their very survival with cavalier indifference.

### Bookshelf Explorer

You may be surprised to hear that your bookshelves will very possibly interest your teen. Give him free rein, even if—especially if—there are

books that are way too mature for him. He is going to come across these subjects anyway. It can be reassuring to know that he might first encounter certain aspects of the adult world on his parents' bookshelf rather than somewhere else. And here's another secret teenagers like to keep from you: They may actually be interested in finding out about you and your life, much as an anthropologist is interested in the ways of the ancient Mayas. Of course, they will never tell you that outright! Browsing your bookshelf, your teenager will probably be relieved to note that you're not so perfect and may need a guide to managing anxiety, or that you, too, indulge in escape reading.

## Keep Books in the Conversation

Just as you routinely ask your kids about their day (which may get you minimal response, but you still keep asking) or talk about the latest Netflix series, regularly ask your kids what they're reading, whether for school or for pleasure. Talk with your spouse at dinner about what *you're* reading. Acknowledge your teenager's maturity and sophistication in this way, and welcome her questions and input, even if she hasn't read the book.

## Defer to the Experts

For any age reader, a good first stop when looking for book recommendations is a librarian or experienced bookseller, but these conversations can especially pay off for parents of teenagers. That's partly because of how your involvement in your child's life has changed now that he's beyond the elementary school years—you probably have less contact with his friends' parents and teachers than you did when he was younger, so the book recommendations and support for fostering his reading you got in those years might be slowing down. Make an effort to have real conversations with a few of these amazing professionals about your son, explaining his seeming lack of interest in reading books as well as his specific personality and interests. Ask what books out there might break through to him. You might also find help in some unexpected places: Stores like Urban Outfitters, for example, that cultivate a hip, young clientele will often stock a book or two that is age appropriate and will make your child's eyes light up for reasons you do not quite fathom but should trust.

# When Teenagers Take Reading Time-Outs

Let's say you've done everything possible to help your child become a passionate reader, and it's worked beautifully. All through elementary school and into the beginning of middle school, she's defined herself through her favorite books, sought out new ones, reread favorites. Then out of the blue, it all seems to shut down. The girl who once plowed through five- and ten-book series like so many pieces of candy has not voluntarily opened a book in weeks. Months. Is this the end? Was it all for naught?

Reader, this happened to Maria. At 13, her daughter took a time-out from reading that lasted almost a year. It was a tough time in her life—she'd moved to a new town and was dealing with middle-school friendship drama, along with an extreme case of adolescent angst. Maria was distraught, until an expert in adolescent psychology explained that teenagers quite often abruptly abandon some of their childhood interests— usually temporarily. They are, after all, in the process of constructing a *new* identity and many do that by creating a kind of "clean slate." Everything that reminds them of their childish self is suddenly unappealing, boring, embarrassing. For Maria's daughter, that meant not just the books she read when she was younger, but *all* books. Instead of reading, she spent her free time doing other things—

listening to music and making playlists, experimenting with thrift-shop clothes and makeup, exploring her new town.

Also, as this psychologist explained, there is only so much space in a teenager's—or anyone's—brain. Figuring out a whole new social and academic landscape, processing physical and emotional changes, adjusting to their new understanding of the world around them—that all takes mental energy, and a teenager may simply have none left over to start a new book, keep playing the piano, or take part in other activities that used to happily take up his brain space. They may be so absorbed with their *own* stories that it's hard to get embroiled in those of others.

If your teenager was a reader as a child but is suddenly showing no interest in reading, our best advice is simply to be patient. Respect where he is right now.

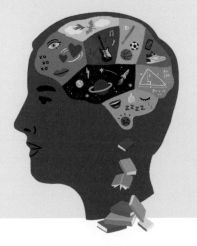

If it seems natural, continue to seek out books you think he may like, and bring them to him or leave them in his room. Maybe it's the YA bestseller that you heard is going to be made into a movie starring an actor you know he likes. Or try some new genres that might spark a new interest: a grown-up thriller or a trendy mystery. But try to remain absolutely unattached to the idea of whether he is reading them. It's his life to live, after all—he's the one writing the story of who he is. Remember that he still lives in a book-filled home, with parents who are readers, and that his history of reading, the books he grew up on, the culture of reading he was exposed to—all of those are indelible parts of that story. None of that ever goes away.

Just when you've finally mastered faux nonchalance about it, your teenager's nonreading spell might come to an end. When Maria's daughter was packing for sleepaway camp, she grabbed all of her Harry Potter books, saying, "I'm going to reread all of them this summer." Soon after that she raced through *The Hate U Give*, and it wasn't long before Maria almost gasped as her daughter flopped down on the sofa with a copy of Stephen King's almost nine-hundred-page *11/22/63* she brought home from the library.

## What to Look For: Young Adult

### Realism Reigns

Literary trends emerge strongly in young adult books, as in everything else. Paranormal stories dominated some previous decades and still have a big presence, but realism in the vein of John Green's megahit *The Fault in Our Stars*, about two teenage cancer patients who fall in love, is going strong as well. These are often the kinds of books that used to be labeled "problem novels"—books that deal with challenging life issues in a realistic way that allows readers to work through their own. Remember that although many of the situations characters in realistic YA books face are disturbing— eating disorders, drug abuse and other forms of self-harm, suicide, mental illness, abusive relationships, every possible kind of untimely death—these books can have incredible value. Whether your child or a friend is going through a similar situation or it's something everyone's whispering about at school, books offer the chance to gain compassion, insight, and even simple knowledge about the darker challenges of adolescence.

### A Medal That Matters

Though not as well known as the Newbery or the Caldecott, the Michael L. Printz Award is also given by the American Library Association and is conferred exclusively on young adult literature. Unlike those other awards, the Printz is not limited to books by American authors. Previous winners have included Meg Rosoff's evocative *How I Live Now*, about an American girl visiting London who's caught in a war with an unnamed enemy, and Paolo Bacigalupi's intelligent post-apocalyptic fantasy *Ship Breaker*.

### Wide-Ranging Diversity

Publishers of YA have become especially mindful of diversity—and their teenage readers are gobbling up so-called Own Voices books, written not just *about* people of color, people with disabilities, women, or members of the LGBTQ community, but by them as well. Diverse authors such as Sabaa Tahir, Jason Reynolds, and Tomi Adeyemi have become superstars whose fans wait eagerly for their next book and greet them rapturously at public appearances. Whatever your teenager's gender, sexuality, or ethnic background, he can benefit from reading YA books by a range of authors, with diverse characters, reflecting the world today's young people are inheriting.

### Visual Books for Teens

Bookstores routinely put large-scale, art-heavy books on sale, and they can be a great way to tempt more visually oriented teenagers to turn pages and get absorbed in a text. A stunning book of photographs from Asia or Africa, say, or a volume on graffiti artists can open the eyes of an adolescent and allow him to think outside his world in a whole new way.

When you're looking for visual books, keep your child's interests in mind, whether it's sports statistics or photography or World War II history. Numbers-oriented kids might especially love books with lots of infographics, charts, and maps. Many curious teenagers will lose themselves in books that wield scientific facts in an adventuresome, visual way, like Randall Munroe's *What If?*, which balances text and illustration in a way that appeals to many teen readers.

## The Right Book, at the Right Moment

Broadly speaking, young adult literature is for ages 12 to 18, but that's not the whole story. Everyone knows that a 13-year-old seventh grader and a 16-year-old tenth grader are very different animals, and although some books are great for both those beasts, others are really, really not. To a certain degree, you can look to your own teenager to know what books are right for her, but there are places to turn for help. Publishers will label works as being 14 and up or 15 and up, especially books that deal with realistic violence (including suicide) or ones that include graphic sexual scenes or themes. These ages are often not marked on the books themselves, but if you ask a knowledgeable bookseller or librarian, check Goodreads or Common Sense Media reviews, or look at information available on online retailer sites, you can find the recommended age range.

## Flights of Fantasy

The middle-grade reader who loved fantasy will find sophisticated offerings in YA, where the heroes and heroines are often fascinatingly complicated people, and the worlds they inhabit are deeply complex. Your Madeleine L'Engle fan may morph into a reader of Ursula K. Le Guin or Patrick Ness or Diana Wynne Jones. Fantasy and science fiction can look like pure pleasure reading, but these stories work on multiple levels. Some kids prefer to engage with characters who are dealing with, say, bullying, gender identity, and racism outside the confines of the all-too-real world readers themselves live in. Often, these very issues are worked on and resolved in fantastical realms.

## Look at Your Shelves Through Your Teenager's Eye

If you're one of those super-organized people who has books alphabetized by author or color coded or shelved by subject, congratulations. Your work is done here. If you're like the rest of us, having a teenager at home might offer a chance to lightly organize your books. Your child may be more apt to consider leaping to more challenging books if finding the right one isn't in itself a challenge. It could be as simple as keeping fiction in one area, nonfiction in another, or maybe creating a section just for books under three hundred pages, or setting aside a shelf of books you think he would especially enjoy. Even just pointing out where you keep your Stephen Kings.

## Give Certain Books Attention

Think of your shelves the way you might envision the most alluring bookshop. Turn certain books face out that your daughter may find appealing. Arrange a stack of books about animals on the coffee table if she recently spoke about animal rights or becoming a veterinarian. Showcase books about the civil rights movement if your son recently brought up the subject. It's all about creating opportunity, both for reading and for good conversation.

## When and Which?

As vibrant as today's YA scene is, many teenagers—especially as they approach their junior and senior years of high school—tire of reading books that foreground the teenage point of view and are set in the world of their age peers. Who can blame them? We think that in addition to YA, teenagers benefit from some aspirational reading that is not assigned to them by a teacher. And sometimes, they want to check out grown-up genres and escapist reading, too. Many kids find their way into the world of adult books all on their own, but for others, parents can play a powerful role. Consider steering your teenager to a grown-up book with teen appeal—one he is unlikely to be assigned for class. The possibilities are pretty much endless. One place to start is with a teen-friendly classic she may already have heard about, such as *Catch-22*, *The Hitchhiker's Guide to the Galaxy*, or *The Group*. If you haven't read them for a long time yourself, give them a quick perusal. In this post-MeToo era, for example, *Lolita* may shock you with its straight-up depiction of an evil pedophile and his precocious, manipulative victim. Rest assured that a teenager growing up today will likely be shocked, too. Maria's teenage daughter was astounded and outraged that once upon a time, a warped person like Humbert Humbert could operate practically out in the open.

## Go with Genre

Genre is an especially great entry point into adult fiction, whether it's legal thrillers by John Grisham or horror by Dean Koontz. Start a conversation with your teenager about which genre he finds most appealing, and help him find those books. But seriously consider reading them first, or at the very least, check out online reviews. (Pamela felt fairly nauseated when she realized halfway through her tween son's reading of Stephen

King's *It* that it isn't all just scary clowns; the novel includes an orgy among 12-year-olds as well.) And remember: A teenager who enjoys King and Koontz may also learn to appreciate classic short fiction by Edgar Allan Poe or H. P. Lovecraft.

## Science Fiction as Gateway

Science fiction classics by the greats—Isaac Asimov, Jules Verne, Octavia E. Butler, H. G. Wells, Ursula K. Le Guin, Ray Bradbury—are especially appealing to kids who gravitate toward video games, science, and technology. But there is much more to science fiction. Le Guin and Butler, for example, are considered among the most powerful feminist tale spinners of all time. All teenagers can appreciate the evocative writing, expansive imagination, and often searing social commentary embedded in the best science fiction books, so consider recommending them to your teenager even if science is not her favorite subject. Then introduce her to contemporary grown-up writers in those genres, such as N. K. Jemisin and Naomi Novik.

## The Benefits of Biography

Teenagers are grappling with their identity and their place in the world, which makes them ripe for stories about how other people have figured out their own lives. Memoir, autobiography, and biography can be the best kind of motivation. They can also encourage a child to take a good hard look at himself, and function as a kind of self-help: It's instructive and reassuring to learn about how other people have overcome challenges and made their way in the world. If your child is interested in computers, you might suggest Walter Isaacson's biography of Steve Jobs or a book about the history of the internet. Sports and history buffs have plenty of fodder. Find biographies of people who share your child's ethnic or racial or religious

heritage. Teenagers like to read about other people who look like them, mirror their experiences or feelings, and understand the communities they live in, but they may just as frequently be drawn to the stories of people who couldn't be more different and relish the chance to vicariously experience the kinds of challenges they themselves never will.

### The Enduring Power of Comics and Graphic Novels

Many of the great works by comics artists were, and are, written for adults, but teenagers are perfectly equipped to appreciate them, too. Art Spiegelman's *Maus* and Marjane Satrapi's *Persepolis*, both written with an adult audience in mind, are included in many high school curricula. Many more excellent graphic novels and memoirs are not published as YA but might speak to your teenager, like Alison Bechdel's *Fun Home*, David Small's *Stitches* and *Home After Dark*, and David Carlson and Landis Blair's *The Hunting Accident*. As always, a more visual young reader will respond to graphic novels with an interest he rarely shows for text-heavy books.

## Be Wary Of

### Pale Imitations

Every hit spawns dozens of often less compelling copycats, and helpfully, you can usually tell by the cover. So if it looks like a great Rainbow Rowell novel—the same typeface or color scheme on the cover, even a similar-looking photo representing the main character—you may want to check the reviews before snapping it up for your choosy teenager.

### Condescension

Whether it was the science-oriented bestsellers of Michael Crichton, the racy adventures of Sidney Sheldon, the breathy romances of Judith Krantz, you probably spent plenty of adolescent hours reading "trashy" adult books. Your kids deserve the same opportunity. If you are a literary-minded type yourself and feel tempted to weigh in on the "quality" of your teenager's reading material, just don't—save your disapproval for vaping, not books.

### An Unfamiliar Label Such as "New Adult"

"New adult" is a label for books considered a notch older than YA, generally because of sexually explicit content. Truth be told, only a small number of books are being published with this designation, but a few authors, like Jennifer L. Armentrout, Richelle Mead, and Cora Carmack, have built loyal fan bases. Although a new-adult book may be great for your older teenager who's curious about life in the later college years and beyond, a younger teenager might be put off or intimidated. Many of these books read like erotica for older teens and twentysomethings, so consider reading one yourself before making a gift of one to your younger teenager. (Frankly, these are the kinds of books most teenagers feel more comfortable selecting on their own.) If it's a book she's requested, it might be a good way to jump-start a conversation about sex and relationships.

## Our Young Adult Novel Picks for Reality Fans

**The Book Thief**
**Markus Zusak**
Historical fiction at its best and most emotionally compelling, starring a girl who copes with life under the Nazis by stealing books.

**Jane, the Fox & Me**
**Fanny Britt,**
**illustrated by Isabelle Arsenault**
A lonely teenage girl tormented by mean kids takes refuge in reading *Jane Eyre* and finds silent communion with a fox. This beautiful graphic

novel about imaginative resilience also shows that true friendship is worth the wait. It is quite short and reads on the younger side of YA but with a sophisticated tone.

**Between Shades of Gray**
**Ruta Sepetys**
This powerful and well-researched novel explores the horrors of Stalinist Russia through the eyes of a 15-year-old Lithuanian girl. No writer brings history to life as intensely as Sepetys does. For the record: This elegant book was published before *Fifty Shades of Grey* and is not to be confused with that bestselling paean to S&M. (It was also published as a grown-up book in its European editions.)

## The Hired Girl
**Laura Amy Schlitz**

A 14-year-old Christian girl, tired of being a drudge on her cruel father's farm, sets off for the city in search of education, art, and love, finding shelter and employment with a kind Jewish family. Set convincingly in 1914, this novel has heart and smarts, daring to explore questions of religion, feminism, loyalty, and belonging.

## The Hate U Give
**Angie Thomas**

The bestseller, written in response to the Black Lives Matter movement, lives up to the hype, with the engagingly told story of a black girl named Starr, a student at a mostly white private school, who witnesses an unarmed friend being shot by a police officer and has to decide how far to go to pursue justice for her friend and for her community. And there's an equally compelling movie!

## Picture Me Gone
**Meg Rosoff**

Mila is unusually sensitive and perceptive for a teenager, so when her dad's best friend is missing, she goes to help solve the mystery—but even she can't see the full truth until it's almost too late. An unforgettable look at the complex relationships between teens and adults.

## The Westing Game
**Ellen Raskin**

A reclusive millionaire names sixteen heirs in his will, setting up a puzzle that the heirs must solve. A modern classic and a wry, mind-bending mystery that a child as young as 10 can get into, but may be best suited for younger teens.

## We Were Liars
**E. Lockhart**

A gripping puzzle of a novel, featuring a girl named Cadence who spends summers with her cousins on their grandfather's island. Something is gravely wrong in this seemingly privileged world, but trust us, you won't know what it is until the jaw-dropping end.

## Monster
**Walter Dean Myers**

Written in the form of a journal and a screenplay by a teenager facing prison for being the lookout during a fatal robbery, this classic explores the adolescent mind while it probes eternal questions of culpability and mercy as well as our broken juvenile justice system.

## My Sister Rosa
**Justine Larbalestier**

In this psychological thriller, a teenager suspects his younger sister is not just naughty and manipulative but a true psychopath. Searingly intelligent and suspenseful.

# Our YA Novel Picks for Fantasy Fans

### Graceling
**Kristin Cashore**
Katsa lives in a world where selected people are given a Grace, a special talent that can be anything from mind reading to fighting. Katsa's is killing. The novel also features a heart-thumping (but relatively chaste) love story.

### The Giver
**Lois Lowry**
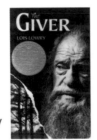
Exploring human connections in a post-apocalyptic world, this ground-breaking, finely written 1994 Newbery Medalist started the current wave of dystopian YA and is now considered a classic of the genre.

### The Dark Is Rising series
**Susan Cooper**
Will Stanton, age 11, finds out he is the last of the "Old Ones." Infused with Arthurian legend and Celtic mythology, this classic British series won multiple awards when it was first published, for good reason.

### The Diviners
**Libba Bray**
A teenage girl with a secret, supernatural power is sent off to New York City during the Roaring Twenties. Intricately plotted and deeply engrossing.

### Scythe
**Neal Shusterman**
In a future in which all evils, even death, have been vanquished, certain individuals are taught the "art of death." Shusterman's smart dystopian tales always raise the kinds of complicated moral questions teenagers love, such as, Can killing be necessary? There is an equally great sequel, *Thunderhead*. Also check out Shusterman's Unwind Dystology, a dark futuristic thriller series along the lines of *1984*.

### The Hazel Wood
**Melissa Albert**
When 17-year-old Alice's mother is stolen away into the mysterious fantasy realm of her late grandmother's cult-classic novel, Alice must enter the dark fairy-tale world herself. This beguiling first novel quickly made its way onto bestseller lists, with its intriguing central mystery and twisted-fairy-tale echoes.

### His Dark Materials series
**Philip Pullman**
In Lyra's world, every human has a daemon—a creature that reflects the core essence of its human companion. (And what kid wouldn't be drawn to that idea?) A modern Narnia-like classic, this intricate, elegant trilogy, beginning with *The Golden Compass*, is smart, challenging, and provocative. It's more

demanding than most YA lit—and also especially rewarding.

### The Shadow and Bone trilogy AND The Six of Crows novels
**Leigh Bardugo**

Set in the especially well-drawn Russian-tinged world of Ravka, where Grisha, the magical military elite, dominate, these gritty, smart, twisty tales are positively bewitching. Note: The characters can be morally ambiguous, and Bardugo's stories deal with sex trafficking, drug dealing, and criminality.

### Children of Blood and Bone
**Tomi Adeyemi**

A West African–inspired epic fantasy about a world where clan- and color-based oppression have gone to the extreme, this opener to a dark dystopian series was an immediate critical and popular hit. The action unfolds in cinematic fashion, infused with timely themes of injustice, equality, discrimination, and rebellion.

### An Ember in the Ashes series
**Sabaa Tahir**

An orphan. A soldier. A sword-and-sand adventure filled with political intrigue, a touch of romance, and a dash of the supernatural, this sweeping series wins praise for its well-drawn characters and fine detail.

## Our Adult Novel Picks for Teenagers

Nearly all of these books have been adapted into movies, presenting great opportunities for family viewing and discussion.

### Never Let Me Go
**Kazuo Ishiguro**

What better way to lure a teenage dystopia fan than with one of the finest modern renditions of the genre? Nobel Prize winner Ishiguro (*The Remains of the Day*) poses a world in which human clones are harvested for organs.

### The Lovely Bones
**Alice Sebold**

Told from the perspective of a murdered 14-year-old girl, now in heaven, this massive bestseller appeals to all ages but perhaps especially to smart, sensitive teenagers for its wise, clear-eyed portrayal of adolescence.

## 1984
**George Orwell**

The progenitor of all modern dystopian tales, this classic political parable will appeal to teenagers with its dark premise and doomed love story.

## Slaughterhouse-Five
**Kurt Vonnegut**

There was a time when all teenagers went through a Vonnegut phase, and for good reason: He's funny, wise, and appealing in that uncle-you're-not-supposed-to-hang-out-with way. The story of Billy Pilgrim and the bombing of Dresden, with all its satirical humor and heartbreak, is his very best.

## Catch-22
**Joseph Heller**

Another great antiwar novel of the same era as Vonnegut's, Heller's classic centers on Yossarian, a bombardier who fears people are trying to kill him—because it's wartime, and they are. Terrifying, hilarious, and impossible to forget your first reading.

## The Princess Bride
**William Goldman**

Yes, the movie is fantastic. So is the book, which some argue is even better. For every obvious reason—giants, a princess, a forbidden romance, pirates, swordplay—this is a book kids will want to grab off your shelf. They'll be reading aloud to *you*.

## Ender's Game
**Orson Scott Card**

A military sci-fi adventure set in space, this grown-up genre novel is probably even better adored by teens. A close brother-and-sister pair, an elite team of gamers, an interstellar war, a conspiracy. (Avoid, alas, all the sequels, which fail to match the original; the movie isn't great either, which can spark a conversation about what makes a successful adaptation.)

## The Joy Luck Club
**Amy Tan**

This massive bestselling intergenerational epic about four Chinese mothers and their Chinese American daughters recounts the eternal and universal drama of the mother-daughter relationship while describing specific aspects of Chinese and immigrant culture with wit and psychological insight.

## The Bell Jar
**Sylvia Plath**

Do all teen girls go through a Plath phase? No, but a certain moody, dreamy, creative, poetically inclined child inevitably does. Plath's autobiographical novel about a young woman's emotional breakdown seems to touch the same nerve as books about suicide, eating disorders, addiction, the struggling artist, and the dark side of human nature that has lured teenagers to books like *Go Ask Alice* and *The Three Faces of Eve*. But this one, by the acclaimed poet, is far better written.

### The Stand
**Stephen King**
Which of King's many books is best to start out on and suitable for a teen? Probably the us-against-them apocalyptic classic *The Stand*, which suits an adolescent sensibility just fine. Dead-heat runner-up: *It*, though the orgy toward the end will require some explanation.

## Our Adult Nonfiction Picks For Teenagers

### I Know Why the Caged Bird Sings
**Maya Angelou**

The classic memoir of girlhood as an African American growing up in the small-town South, confronted with racial prejudice and horrific abuse. And yet there is heart and uplift in this story of moving past life's most stinging brutalities.

### The Immortal Life of Henrietta Lacks
**Rebecca Skloot**
This account of how one African American woman's cancer cells spawned a world of scientific discovery and insight will appeal to a wide range of readers, whether their interest is race; science; history; or pure, gut-pummeling, heart-wrenching, human-interest storytelling.

### Persepolis
**Marjane Satrapi**
One of the greatest graphic memoirs ever written, this coming-of-age narra-tive tells the story of a girl growing up in revolution-era Iran, when the shah is overthrown and a world crumbles overnight. And yet, it is full of humor and heart. Adolescents who love an angst-ridden story will love this. A masterpiece. (Note: The protagonist is an unapologetic teenage smoker.)

### The Man Who Mistook His Wife for a Hat
**Oliver Sacks**
One of Sacks's most engaging collec-tions of essays tells the case-study stories of the famed neurologist's mysteriously afflicted patients. Kids as young as 9 can get wrapped up in these moving human mysteries. For anyone interested in suspense, medicine, quirky facts, brain science, even Ripley's Believe It or Not!

### Go Tell It on the Mountain
**James Baldwin**
A landmark coming-of-age-in-Harlem story written in 1953, Baldwin's memoir is considered the modern classic of the genre. The realism and darkness are at the same time lyrical, mesmerizing, inspiring. Also: *Invisible Man* by Ralph Ellison.

### Quackery: A Brief History of the Worst Ways to Cure Everything
**Lydia Kang and Nate Pedersen**
One of those fun reference books for kids who've graduated from big compendiums of strange facts and bizarre records and want a little more hardcore scientific history; this one has a welcome gross-out factor.

### Maus
**Art Spiegelman**
The Jews are mice and the Germans, cats. The publication of this devastating graphic memoir about the son of a Holocaust survivor marked a turning point in which graphic books were celebrated and widely read by a mass audience. Chilling, poignant, masterful.

### What If?: Serious Scientific Answers to Absurd Hypothetical Questions
**Randall Munroe**
This book offers answers to every wacky, seemingly unanswerable question a 5- or 12- or 33-year-old has ever asked, but with actual backup. What if lightning struck every place on earth at the exact same moment? Herewith, the answer.

### Educated
**Tara Westover**
This debut memoir by a woman raised in a rural Idaho family where school, health care, and anything government run are verboten is a searing coming-of-age story that explores what it means to get an education and to extract yourself from a violently dysfunctional family. Another great coming-of-age memoir about the power of education is Jung Chang's *Wild Swans*, a family epic about a grandmother, mother, and daughter in twentieth-century China.

### In Cold Blood
**Truman Capote**
Four family members on a farm in Kansas are brutally murdered one night in 1959. No motive, no clues. The classic true-crime story still holds its grip on readers today and raises all kinds of moral issues that will have teenagers deep-diving into the background story.

# PART FIVE

# More Books to Love

*By Theme and Reading Level*

# FINDING THE RIGHT BOOK AT THE RIGHT TIME

You have a good sense of who your child is, even as she grows and changes. You know whether he always appreciates a funny school story or a heartbreaking animal tale. You know if he's looking for a book about friendship at the moment, or maybe you have a feeling he may need one and not quite know it. And you also know yourself and the ever-evolving needs of your family. When you have a second child on the way, you look out for books about new siblings. Sometimes, we all are dying to find just the right book targeted to a specific interest and age level. With that in mind, in this section we look at books for every age level across a number of subject areas, genres, reader needs, and themes. We've got books for a sensitive boy trying to make friends and books for a teenage girl struggling to keep them. We've got great family read-alouds and great books in audio format for the entire family.

Are these books the best of the best? Not necessarily (though most of them, we would judge, are). What these lists really consist of are our highly personal, idiosyncratic picks. Books that we and our kids have read and relished. Books that have met our kids at the moment they needed them. Books that delivered unexpected and valuable lessons. Books that we read as children ourselves that still hold up, and new books that we read with our kids, or as editors at the *Book Review*, that have stuck with us. Like the rest of the titles we've called out in earlier sections, these are books that we highly recommend for kids at every age and reading level.

They are organized by subject first, and then into three categories—Picture Books, Chapter/Middle-Grade Books, and Young Adult Books. The chapter/middle-grade books include a mix of emerging and independent reader books.

# Books That Make Us Laugh

## PICTURE BOOKS

### Rotten Island
**William Steig**
On this vicious island, where ferocious beasts tear one another apart limb from limb for pleasure, the hardest thing to tolerate is an unexpected flower. But that's the power of beauty.

### The Obstinate Pen
**Frank W. Dormer**
Every stymied writer knows the frustration of not being able to put your thoughts into words, especially when you're still mastering basic pencil skills. In this hilariously absurdist tale, the pen truly has a mind of its own—full of pranks and riotously inappropriate commentary.

### Those Darn Squirrels!
**Adam Rubin,**
**illustrated by Daniel Salmieri**
What is the point of this story about Old Man Fookwire and his beloved birds, and the squirrels who terrorize them? There is none! Other than pure comic bliss. *Robo-Sauce* is another winner by this team, featuring a kid who tries hard to turn himself into a robot and a special foldout ending that will make little heads spin with delight.

### I Want My Hat Back
**Jon Klassen**
A bear has lost his hat. A turtle denies any involvement. Someone is lying. This true original established the author as a children's-book genius, rightly winning a Caldecott Medal. Sly, inventive, and witty. Bonus: There are two follow-ups, *This Is Not My Hat* and *We Found a Hat*.

### I'm Bored
**Michael Ian Black,**
**illustrated by Debbie Ridpath Ohi**
Every parent has heard this phrase a zillion times. Here, a dark-haired lass is complaining, and a talking potato is her adversary. This charming and hilarious story by the comic actor and essayist and his frequent illustrator collaborator will quickly un-bore any reader.

### Battle Bunny
**Jon Scieszka and Mac Barnett,**
**illustrated by Matthew Myers**
Subversive metafiction for older picture book readers from two contemporary children's-book geniuses as an uplifting bunny story is radically defaced and rewritten into an explosive-ridden tale of mayhem. Inspired.

### It's Only Stanley
**Jon Agee**
The Wimbledon family keeps getting woken up by strange noises. But it's only the family dog, Stanley. Little do they know what he's really up to. Kids will roar with laughter. Agee has written and illustrated many other fantastic books— he's a reliable choice when you're looking for smart plus funny.

### The King Who Rained
Fred Gwynne

A classic picture book of common expressions literally translated into absurd images, it taps into kids' boundless enthusiasm for misunderstandings and malapropisms. Just think of the illustrations that go along with these: "Daddy says there are forks in the road." "Mommy says not to bother her when she's playing bridge."

### Snail & Worm AND Snail & Worm Again
Tina Kugler

Let's face it, snails and worms are funny looking, and Kugler plays up the creatures' inherent silliness in these perfectly timed short tales. They work as picture books or giggle-inducing early readers.

### Snappsy the Alligator (Did Not Ask to Be in This Book!)
Julie Falatko,
illustrated by Tim Miller

One of our favorite "meta" picture books, this one features a hilarious bow-tied alligator, and when you discover the identity of the narrator who's talking to him, you will be shocked the first time . . . and still giggle the times after that.

### Read the Book, Lemmings!
Ame Dyckman,
illustrated by Zachariah OHora

This author-illustrator team delivers funny books that feel original both visually and in their wry humor, as in this one about a squad of lemmings on a ship who really should learn to read.

### Can Somebody Please Scratch My Back?
Jory John,
illustrated by Liz Climo

What's worse than an unscratchable itch? A bunch of hapless animals who prove incapable of helping out our (selfish) elephant antihero. A lesson on generosity and gratitude that's more bitingly funny than syrupy sweet. Runners-up by Jory John: *Goodnight Already!*, *I Love You Already!*, and others featuring the same duck and bear duo, with illustrations by Benji Davies.

### Brief Thief
Michaël Escoffier,
illustrated by Kris Di Giacomo

This outrageously funny picture book delivers the laughs again and again. A lizard needs to *go* and, not finding toilet paper handy in the great outdoors, swipes a pair of underwear hanging from a tree. The voice of his conscience sets in. Hilarity ensues. You can't go wrong with any of the four picture books from this author-illustrator team.

### Someone Farted
Bruce Eric Kaplan

The title alone says it all, but this hilarious story about a mysterious fart in the car first divides, then unites, a family. Told in a matter-of-fact tone that adds to the humor, it's as sweet and heartwarming as a story about flatulence can be. Kaplan, who cartoons as BEK for the *New Yorker*, is fast becoming a picture book star.

### A Perfectly Messed-Up Story
**Patrick McDonnell**
Our hero is trying to tell a really good story when somebody messes up the page. Smears the crayon. Spills juice. Is that peanut butter? It's incredibly annoying and uproariously funny when he naturally throws a fit over the intrusion.

### Samantha on a Roll
**Linda Ashman,**
**illustrated by Christine Davenier**
Told in verse, this charming picture book has a girl trying out new roller skates only to find herself careering downhill, out of control. Accidents, mishaps, crashes, and near-crashes will have everyone shrieking with glee.

### The Very Inappropriate Word
**Jim Tobin,**
**illustrated by Dave Coverly**
This one takes a subject that could invite preachiness and turns it into pure entertainment. Michael loves collecting words like *shenanigans* and *nimbus* until one day, he overhears a word not suitable for repetition. It's written as a scribbly mess of symbols. If only this never happened in real life.

### The Boss Baby
**Marla Frazee**
Far better than the movie that came from it, this Frazee classic features a baby who knows that he is in charge of his family and expects full deference. What could be as ripe for humor (and yet sadly realistic) as that?

### King Baby
**Kate Beaton**
Another baby-in-charge delight. The absurdly cute "hero" looks more like an egg than a human, with a gold crown to boot: "It is good to be king," it says on one page as iPhones snap at his royal highness in fealty.

### Leave Me Alone!
**Vera Brosgol**
The first picture book by Brosgol, author of terrific graphic novels for older kids, this story employs a comic strip–inspired style to tell an invented folktale that feels like it's been around for ages— in a good way.

## CHAPTER BOOKS AND MIDDLE GRADE

### Grandpa's Great Escape
### AND others
**David Walliams,**
**illustrated by Tony Ross**
You're never too young for cheeky, madcap British humor, as the British bestsellers by this duo prove. In this one, Jack is determined to save his beloved, dotty grandpa, currently living in an old folks' home, who sometimes believes he's still a World War II fighter pilot. Walliams's books are well suited for the Wimpy Kid and *13-Story Treehouse* crowd.

### The World According to Humphrey series
**Betty G. Birney**
A classroom hamster with a mind of his own and a willing team of kids who

help him out: Told from the view of Humphrey the Hamster, these tales have Birney wringing a mind-boggling amount of storytelling fun out of a familiar but fresh scenario.

### The Mrs. Piggle-Wiggle series
**Betty MacDonald**
She lives in an upside-down house that smells like freshly baked cookies. But it's not all fun and games with this magical problem-solving neighbor lady. This series was first published in the 1950s, so between laughs, kids may marvel at long-ago ideas of bad behavior. A charming updated take on this world has been published, titled the Missy Piggle-Wiggle series, featuring Mrs. P's niece, written by Ann M. Martin and illustrated by Ben Hatke.

### The Hero's Guide trilogy
**Christopher Healy,**
**illustrated by Todd Harris**
This fractured fairy-tale adventure features four Princes Charmings who are rejected by their princesses. Relatable! They must track down Cinderella and right things gone amok in the kingdom.

### Rump, Red, Jack, AND Grump
**Liesl Shurtliff**
More fractured fairy tales, with fairy-tale characters who are awkward, cranky, and generally down on their luck. *Rump* takes the Rumpelstiltskin story, *Red* is Little Red Riding Hood, and so on. These antiheroes are all the sweeter to root for as they outwit the usual assortment of evildoers.

### Half Magic
**Edward Eager**
Four cousins on summer vacation find a magic coin, but there's a catch: Only half your wish comes true. A timeless mix of humor and adventure, written in the 1950s. Eager followed up with a number of companion books.

### Uncle Shawn and Bill and the Almost Entirely Unplanned Adventure
**A. L. Kennedy**
The well-regarded adult novelist Kennedy's first book for young readers is a zany, clever, and satisfying tale. A handsome badger is captured by—and rescued from—a hilariously clueless and mean-spirited human family.

### The Charlie & Mouse books
**Laurel Snyder,**
**illustrated by Emily Hughes**
Charlie and Mouse are brothers who have the funniest misunderstandings. Family humor is done to perfection in these early chapter books, with simple words and warm illustrations full of winning touches like the mom freaking out in the background.

### The Upside-Down Magic series
**Sarah Mlynowski, Lauren Myracle, and Emily Jenkins**
What if there were a Hogwarts for kids whose magic was "different"? This delightful series about a diverse group learning to live with their "wonky" magic draws a clear line to the challenges real-life kids with special needs face every day, though everyone will

identify as they try to overcome problems like transforming into a creature who's half kitten, half dragon.

### To Be a Cat
**Matt Haig**
A boy named Barney wakes up as a cat, which is not as great as it might sound. Mixes humor and adventure with a sweet lesson about learning to love yourself for who you really are.

### The Secret series
**Pseudonymous Bosch**
Starting with *The Name of This Book Is Secret*, this series has an elusive narrator and mystery-solving kid characters who have a secret, too. Certain kids can't get enough of Bosch's brain-teasing humor.

### The Land of Stories books
**Chris Colfer**
This wildly popular series by the multi-talented Colfer (he's an actor as well) sends modern-day kids into the magical lands of familiar fairy tales. Funny, surprising, and occasionally scary twists ensue.

### The Princess in Black books
**Shannon Hale and Dean Hale, illustrated by LeUyen Pham**
Even if you're wary of princess-themed books, the unlikely adventures of Princess Magnolia and her fierce, black-clad alter ego make tired old tropes about "damsels in distress" do somersaults.

### Everything on a Waffle
**Polly Horvath**
Little Primrose Squarp insists she is not an orphan after her parents disappear at sea, so the town tracks down an eccentric uncle to care for her, with frequent trips to a diner where every dish comes on a waffle. Kooky fun, with a memorable heroine.

### The Lunch Lady books
**Jarrett J. Krosoczka**
Ever wonder what the lunch lady does when she's not serving inedible food? This one solves mysteries—and fights for justice! A graphic series that's as addictive as the best french fries.

### The Joey Pigza series
**Jack Gantos**
Joey's ADHD makes each day a new adventure. But he meets every challenge—and there are many—with crackpot humor.

### Hoot
**Carl Hiaasen**
You may know Hiaasen from his pitch-perfect adult comic novels set in Florida, and his books for kids are equally nutty and smart. In this one, a boy tries to save a colony of endangered owls who've taken up unwelcome residence at a pancake restaurant. Hiaasen has written several other related stories, with more to come.

### Mr. Popper's Penguins
**Florence and Richard Atwater**
A bored house painter who longs to be a polar explorer comes to own a fleet of

penguins, so he trains them to perform and takes them on tour. A classic of absurdist humor.

### Frindle
**Andrew Clements,**
**illustrated by Brian Selznick**
Just to bug his teacher, a mischief-making boy invents a new word for pen—*frindle*—and soon it spreads across the country. Sly fun for word lovers and what-if thinkers.

### To Night Owl from Dogfish
**Holly Goldberg Sloan and Meg Wolitzer**
Two 11-year-old girls—one in California, one in New York—are horrified to learn that their dads are dating each other and have secretly sent the girls to the same summer camp to "meet" by accident. By the time this hilarious book, told all in emails, turns into a gay-dad *Parent Trap*, you'll be laughed out and may even shed a tear of joy at the ending.

## YA

### Beauty Queens
**Libba Bray**
The contestants in a Teen Dream beauty contest are stranded on a desert island after a plane crash. Aren't you dying to know what happens next? Also see Bray's *Going Bovine*.

### Noggin
**John Corey Whaley**
Travis wakes up one day with his severed head reattached to someone else's body (a miracle of modern surgery). Among other problems to be resolved: Is his old girlfriend still his girlfriend? Whaley's revved-up, somewhat raunchy storytelling hurtles along into crazier and crazier places.

### Grasshopper Jungle
**Andrew Smith**
If Kurt Vonnegut had written YA, it might have looked a lot like Smith's books. Bizarro, brainy fun involving giant insects running wild after the apocalypse.

### Nothing
**Annie Barrows**
Two high school sophomores with lives that are totally boring decide to write down everything that happens for a year, to prove their point. The results are unexpected, and the humor is sly and sneaky.

### When Dimple Met Rishi
**Sandhya Menon**
Two Indian American teenagers discover that their parents are angling for an arranged marriage between them. Gross! Menon works the intersection of Indian and American culture for delightful, slow-burning teen humor.

# Tearjerkers

## PICTURE BOOKS

### Knuffle Bunny Free
**Mo Willems**
The third volume in the Knuffle Bunny trilogy is especially moving as little Trixie outgrows her lovey. Yes, it's a big step for Trixie; it's one for most parents as well.

### Miss Rumphius
**Barbara Cooney**
Little Alice makes a promise to make the world a more beautiful place. A seed of an idea is planted and, when she is an old woman, blossoms into a splendid plan that we see coming to fruition in the weepy ending.

### Otto: The Autobiography of a Teddy Bear
**Tomi Ungerer**
A boy with a gold star on his lapel gives his teddy bear to his best friend when he's suddenly taken away (you can see where this is going). The teddy bear goes on to live a life of his own, eventually immigrating to America and, ultimately, reuniting with his loved ones.

### Sylvester and the Magic Pebble
**William Steig**
A boy is suddenly transformed into a rock by a magic pebble while his parents despair over their loss. Justly winning the Caldecott Medal, this story of love and perseverance will charm children while wreaking havoc on their grown-up companions.

### Missing Mommy
**Rebecca Cobb**
One of the most profound and soulful works about a child coping with a parent's death, this book centers on a young girl's conversations with her father with honesty and heart, told in simple, powerful language that children will recognize as their own.

### Love
**Matt de la Peña,**
**illustrated by Loren Long**
A poetic tribute to love in all its difficulties and triumphs, this book reassures children and casts an emotional spell over many parents.

### Mama's Nightingale
**Edwidge Danticat,**
**illustrated by Leslie Staub**
Danticat writes critically acclaimed books for grown-ups, and her picture book debut is a heart wrencher: A young girl misses her mother, who has been detained by immigration authorities, but takes solace in listening to cassettes of Haitian folklore her mother sends her from jail.

### Boats for Papa
**Jessixa Bagley**
A young beaver builds little sailboats and launches them in the river for his papa, who is gone. This exquisitely sensitive book is about handling a loss that is never specified and could be death or abandonment or something else.

## The Heart and the Bottle
### Oliver Jeffers
A little girl loses someone very special to her, so she puts her heart in a bottle to protect it . . . until she realizes it's time to live again in this story about mourning and moving on, leavened by Jeffers's always mysteriously captivating art.

## The Lion and the Bird
### Marianne Dubuc
In this achingly beautiful book, a solitary lion rescues a wounded little bird and nurses it to health, discovering the joy of companionship. Then he learns another lesson about friendship when it's time to say goodbye so the bird can rejoin its flock.

# CHAPTER BOOKS AND MIDDLE GRADE

## Wonder
### R. J. Palacio
A boy with a facial deformity enters a mainstream school. This stunning debut novel will break and then mend all hearts, guaranteed. Bonus: The movie is as good as a novel adaptation gets—but for this one especially, make sure your kid reads the book first!

## Ms. Bixby's Last Day
### John David Anderson
Three troubled boys at the center of this novel make a special picnic for the extraordinary, cancer-stricken teacher who may not ever return to their classroom. An unforgettable look at the emotional lives of boys.

## Pax
### Sara Pennypacker, illustrated by Jon Klassen
A boy whose mother has died raises an orphaned fox kit as a pet, but when his father is called up for military duty, he's forced to release the unprepared animal into the wild. With alternating chapters from the fox's and the boy's point of view, it makes a heartbreaking case for the human-animal bond and, not incidentally, the inhumanity of war.

## Bridge to Terabithia
### Katherine Paterson
The tears come at the very sad ending of this classic about two best friends, a boy and a girl, who escape their everyday lives into a made-up world of their own.

## When Friendship Followed Me Home
### Paul Griffin
A rescued dog and a former foster kid who takes daily refuge in the library form an unbreakable bond in this story about learning to trust. There's a perfectly happy ending, but the tears may keep coming anyway.

## The Seventh Wish
### Kate Messner
Messner beautifully weaves fantasy and realism in this timely story of a girl who meets a wishing fish. All life's problems seem about to be solved, until her older sister's opioid addiction brings a sad reality crashing in.

## Where the Red Fern Grows
**Wilson Rawls**

This tale of a young boy in the Ozarks and his two hunting dogs has brought tears to the eyes of animal-loving readers for decades, for good reason. It's sad as heck but also as lovely and poignant as a star-filled summertime sky.

## The Night Diary
**Veera Hiranandani**

This novel presents the history of India's Partition through the eyes of a half-Muslim, half-Hindu 12-year-old girl forced to relocate with her family. In Hiranandani's carefully detailed prose, the long, hot journey comes to heart-wrenching life.

## Orbiting Jupiter
**Gary D. Schmidt**

A 13-year-old boy in and out of detention and foster care finds out he's fathered a child, whom he's determined to see. Schmidt is the master of telling difficult stories that somehow glimmer with hope.

## The Miraculous Journey of Edward Tulane
**Kate DiCamillo**

The utterly mesmerizing tale of a vain and selfish china rabbit who learns to love after falling off a cruise ship. Edward's suspenseful adventures take him from owner to owner, building to an almost unbearably poignant ending.

# YA

## Salt to the Sea
**Ruta Sepetys**

At the end of World War II, four desperate young men and women from across Germany, Poland, and Lithuania band together to escape the advancing Red Army, hoping to board a ship called the *Wilhelm Gustloff*. Their fates entwine with one of the greatest maritime disasters in history in this impeccably researched, compassionate, devastating story.

## The Fault in Our Stars
**John Green**

This improbable and tragic love story between two young cancer patients captures adolescent love so wrenchingly, it will leave teenagers deeply moved and adult readers heartbroken—in a good way. It's a rite-of-passage read for many teenagers. Those who came of age in the eighties: Think Norma Klein's *Sunshine* but specifically for teens.

## Speak
**Laurie Halse Anderson**

A pioneering, powerful treatment of rape in YA, this essential book tells the story of Melinda, who gains the courage to speak out about the violent attack that happened to her at a high school party, and in so doing, overcomes her subsequent feelings of depression and social isolation. The excellent graphic novel version may make the story and the nuances of consent it examines easier to truly comprehend for some readers, especially boys.

## Kissing in America
**Margo Rabb**
This sensitive novel is mostly about infatuation and the lengths we'll go to for a first love, but it also deftly captures the numbness of grief and the pain of a deceased parent's absence.

## An Episode of Sparrows
**Rumer Godden**
Set in bombed-out World War II London, this novel focuses on a hidden garden, a posse of neighborhood children, and a bitter older woman who must decide whether to open her heart to an orphaned child's plight. Brief and deeply affecting.

## The Chocolate War
**Robert Cormier**
Menacing rituals at an all-boys prep school go under the microscope in this classic, which traces one teenager's difficult path to standing up to peer pressure. Makes you think and feel intensely, as does another by Cormier, *I Am the Cheese*.

## Piecing Me Together
**Renée Watson**
In this powerfully moving novel, a poor, African American girl at an elite private school learns to navigate the rules of her two worlds. But when she's made to participate in a mentoring program, she rebels, tired of being the one who needs "help."

## Illegal
**Eoin Colfer and Andrew Donkin, illustrated by Giovanni Rigano**
This graphic novel about an orphaned African boy's perilous journey across the desert and the sea to safety in Europe reverberates with tragedy and heroism. It's written and drawn to perfection by the experienced team behind the popular Artemis Fowl graphic novels, who did deep research into the migrant crisis.

## They Both Die at the End
**Adam Silvera**
This stirring futuristic story grapples with death from every angle. In a world in which you're informed of your last day alive on that day, two friends are brought together by an app to share theirs, and meet for one last adventure.

## Anna and the Swallow Man
**Gavriel Savit**
During World War II, a 7-year-old Polish girl is left alone when her father is taken by the Germans, but a mysterious man she calls the Swallow Man takes her to hide out in the forest. Full of myth, magic, and humanity.

## Endangered
**Eliot Schrefer**
A girl must rescue a group of bonobos from a sanctuary when a violent coup overtakes the Congo. A heart-stopping story about caring, survival, and what we owe to animals.

# Heart Warmers

## PICTURE BOOKS

### Dreamers
**Yuyi Morales**
Morales's story of emigrating with her infant son to the United States from Mexico makes their difficult cultural transition into a journey toward wonder and acceptance, culminating in a tribute to the library where they both fell in love with children's books. Her collage-style multimedia art is rich and enchantingly detailed, including tiny replicas of hundreds of classic picture books.

### I Must Have Bobo!
**Eileen Rosenthal,**
**illustrated by Marc Rosenthal**
Earl the cat keeps swiping a boy's monkey lovey. He doesn't mean any harm; he just can't help it. With charming, spare drawings, this sweet ode to the things that comfort us ends well. Two subsequent volumes are also winners.

### Sidewalk Flowers
**JonArno Lawson,**
**illustrated by Sydney Smith**
This wordless but poetic tale about a little girl who collects flowers as she walks home with her distracted dad will make you smile at the realization of how simple it is to find beauty and to be kind. Smith—one of our very favorite illustrators—seems to have a mysterious power to put you in a good mood.

### The Storm Whale
**Benji Davies**
A little boy named Noi, who lives alone with his fisherman dad, finds a beached baby whale and takes it home in this simple but mesmerizing story about loneliness, connection, and tuning in to the people we love. The follow-up is equally enchanting: *The Storm Whale in Winter*.

### Crown: An Ode to the Fresh Cut
**Derrick Barnes,**
**illustrated by Gordon C. James**
This debut won a slew of awards for its jazzy, jubilant celebration of the ritual and power of an African American boy's trip to the local barbershop.

### The Otis books
**Loren Long**
Sure, Otis is a tractor who lives on a farm surrounded by animals, but at heart these are stories about friendship and cooperation, with a mysterious emotional undertow. And lush, appealing artwork.

### The Rabbit Listened
**Cori Doerrfeld**
A child's carefully built block construction is knocked over, and a series of animals come with their respective bits of advice and consolation, none of it quite right. But the rabbit comes and sits quietly, just listening until the child decides on the best solution. A thing of beauty.

### This Plus That: Life's Little Equations
**Amy Krouse Rosenthal, illustrated by Jen Corace**
One of Krouse Rosenthal's many gems, this simple story seems to be about math but is really about life itself. "Chores ÷ everyone = family." "Good days + bad days = real life."

### Pie Is for Sharing
**Stephanie Parsley Ledyard, illustrated by Jason Chin**
An old-fashioned picnic on the Fourth of July just begs to be capped off by a summer dessert. A simple story about sharing is also one about pluralism, community, and the inclusive, all-American way.

### Where's My Teddy?
**Jez Alborough**
"Eddie's off to find his teddy. Eddie's teddy's name is Freddy." A boy and a bear each lose their teddy bears in the great big forest. After an initially frightful encounter, they find each other and a new friendship. Two adorable spin-offs, *It's the Bear!* and *My Friend Bear*, follow the characters as they age but still hold on to their respective teddies.

## CHAPTER BOOKS AND MIDDLE GRADE

### Pinny in Summer AND Pinny in Fall
**Joanne Schwartz, illustrated by Isabelle Malenfant**
These charming, very brief stories about an imaginative, independent little girl who lives by the sea straddle the divide between picture books and chapter books. They're contemporary but have a timeless feel.

### My Happy Life
**Rose Lagercrantz, illustrated by Eva Eriksson**
This sweet story about a girl starting kindergarten with an optimistic outlook, despite having lost her mother, is beautiful and inspiring. With five equally lovely follow-ups, so far.

### The Vanderbeekers of 141st Street
**Karina Yan Glaser**
This biracial family with four kids lives in a Harlem brownstone apartment building and has the kind of warm, funny, character-filled neighborhood life that makes you long to move next door to them. And to read the sequel, *The Vanderbeekers and the Hidden Garden*.

### Secret Sisters of the Salty Sea
**Lynne Rae Perkins**
A transcendent summertime story: Two sisters from the Midwest take their first-ever trip to the beach for a weeklong vacation in which they come to appreciate each other as well as the beauty and majesty of the natural world.

### Tom's Midnight Garden
**Philippa Pearce**
This classic from the 1950s about a boy who discovers a time-travel mechanism in a grandfather clock is full of rich characters and a page-turning plot. A fantastic new graphic

novel version, dazzlingly illustrated by Edith, makes the story come alive in a whole new way.

### The Heart and Mind of Frances Pauley
**April Stevens**
Eleven-year-old Frances is odd. She calls herself "Figgrotten" and has turned her room into a virtual nature museum. She becomes even more solitary after her beloved bus driver passes away, but she learns to connect to a new friend and her older sister. Lovely and encouraging for anyone who feels different.

### The Crossover
**Kwame Alexander**
Twin brothers who are high school basketball stars begin moving apart from each other in this exhilarating, multiple-award-winning novel in verse. A tour de force of language and a memorable story about finding your own way while keeping old bonds strong.

### The Wild Robot
**Peter Brown**
What if a smart robot fell off a ship and was marooned on an island inhabited only by animals? This bestselling novel and its sequel explore nature and technology with uncommon heart and an environmentally aware sensibility.

### Beyond the Bright Sea
**Lauren Wolk**
An orphaned girl and her kind adoptive father set out on a journey to find answers about her past in this vividly told story about the true meaning of family. The emotional resonance of fable, with suspense mixed in.

### Because of Winn-Dixie
**Kate DiCamillo**
One of the great who-rescued-whom stories: A dog is found in a grocery store by a girl struggling to make friends and understand why her mother is gone. Both lives are changed as the two travel around town meeting new people.

## YA

### Nick and Norah's Infinite Playlist
**Rachel Cohn and David Levithan**
A love story, with music—the boy and girl protagonists, each recovering from a broken heart, fall in love by collaborating on the perfect playlist over one very long night.

### Aristotle and Dante Discover the Secrets of the Universe
**Benjamin Alire Sáenz**
Two sad, wary Latino boys who meet at a public pool learn how to let down their guards and embrace the wonders of being alive. A searching, exquisitely told tale of gay teenage experience.

### Skellig
**David Almond**
This soulful, offbeat Printz Award winner is about Michael, a teenager who finds a strange, demanding creature in his garage and is drawn into an ever-increasing mystery: Could the creature be an angel?

## The Earth, My Butt, and Other Big Round Things AND The Universe Is Expanding and So Am I
**Carolyn Mackler**

It is a joy to root for the funny, lovable heroine of these two novels as she comes to accept her plus-size body, speak her own truth, and navigate the sometimes sleazy upper-crust New York City world she lives in.

## The Sun Is Also a Star
**Nicola Yoon**

An exhilarating love story that takes place over the course of one day. A science-loving Jamaican girl about to be deported because of a paperwork error and a Korean American boy meet literally while crossing the street, and must decide whether to follow their hearts after instantly falling for each other.

# Family Stories

## PICTURE BOOKS

### The Day Louis Got Eaten
**John Fardell**

A monster swipes a boy, setting his sister off in hot pursuit on her bicycle. It's refreshing to see a book about sibling teamwork rather than rivalry. The monsters' names alone—the Grabular, the Undersnatch, the Spiney-backed Guzzler, for starters—will have children giggling.

### Hello! Hello!
**Matthew Cordell**

This sweet story about a girl trying to capture the joys of nature and open-ended creativity despite the distractions beckoning her screen-addicted family sends an important message about family members seeing and hearing each other in real life.

### Building Our House
**Jonathan Bean**

This true story about a family of homesteaders building their own house from scratch in the 1970s shows a family working together and appreciating the fruits of their hard labor. Kids will marvel at the step-by-steps of building a home, in every sense of the word. Likewise, Bean's *This Is My Home, This Is My School* is perhaps the best, most joyful depiction of home schooling we've come across.

### This Is the Rope
**Jacqueline Woodson, illustrated by James Ransome**

Award-winning author Woodson weaves a warm story about the African American Great Migration—from 1916 to 1970—cleverly using a common household item to signify the ties that bind families and generations.

### The Seven Silly Eaters
**Mary Ann Hoberman,**
**illustrated by Marla Frazee**

Hoberman's flawless rhyming is matched only by Frazee's marvelous illustrations in this funny tale of an ever-expanding family of picky eaters. With so many characters to engage with, this book invites and rewards repeat readings and close study of the pictures.

### Alexander and the Terrible, Horrible, No Good, Very Bad Day
**Judith Viorst,**
**illustrated by Ray Cruz**

This classic picture book about the everyday traumas of growing up and living in a family introduces Alexander, his two irritating older brothers, and his long-suffering parents who really just don't understand—most of the time. There are three additional Alexander books that follow this one, all loaded with humor and kid-focused empathy.

### Grandpa Green
**Lane Smith**

A tender but unsentimental appreciation of the connections between generations, in which one great-grandpa's long past and faulty memory are all just part of the picture. The stunningly detailed outdoor art, all in the color green, will keep young eyes riveted.

### Nana in the City
**Lauren Castillo**

A tribute to the kind of grandma who takes you to shows, lets you ride in taxis, makes you laugh, and helps you feel less afraid of new things. Warm and wonderful, and winner of a Caldecott Honor.

### Zelda and Ivy
**Laura McGee Kvasnovsky**

These two adventurous and devoted fox sisters don't always get along, but over the course of a half-dozen books, they navigate their sibling dynamics in always surprising and hugely amusing ways.

### Julius, the Baby of the World
**Kevin Henkes**

Why is everyone so enamored of Lilly's new baby brother? After all, "If he was a number, he'd be zero." Henkes captures sibling rivalry with the sensitivity of a child psychologist and an artist. Children will smile, sigh, and laugh with recognition.

## CHAPTER BOOKS AND MIDDLE GRADE

### The Secret Garden
**Frances Hodgson Burnett**

This classic novel, published in 1911 and set at the turn of the previous century, is about the coming-of-age of a rude and unloved little girl and her cousin, who is hidden away and treated as an invalid. Both are eventually redeemed in different ways, healing their family in the process.

### Little Women
**Louisa May Alcott**

What better family story is there than that of Marmee, Father, and their four daughters making their way in New England?

## All-of-a-Kind Family

**Sydney Taylor**

This series of books conveys simple tales about a large Jewish family who live on the Lower East Side of Manhattan in the early twentieth century. They don't have a lot of money, but they're rich in the rewards of tradition and kinship.

## The Penderwicks

**Jeanne Birdsall**

This series focuses on a strongly bonded family of six siblings, joined together by blood, death, and remarriage after divorce. There's something old-fashioned about any big-family story, yet this particular set of stories has a stealthily modern feeling.

## The Best Man

**Richard Peck**

In this gem from the prolific and big-hearted Peck, a fifth grader is asked to be best man at his gay uncle's wedding, to one of the boy's teachers. This book is perhaps the crowning achievement of the late, much-honored author.

## Ling & Ting

**Grace Lin**

Best for ages 6 to 9, the Ling & Ting series of books about spunky twin sisters are a playful look at the trials and joys of twinship, with the bonus of Lin's adorable illustrations.

## The Year of Billy Miller

**Kevin Henkes**

We follow second grader Billy over the course of the year as he navigates school and friendships. The grounding of his family life is the heart of this charming book, which includes a rare realistic school setting for younger boy readers.

## One Crazy Summer

**Rita Williams-Garcia**

This realistic and funny story of three sisters—who travel from Brooklyn to Oakland, California, in 1968 to meet the mother who abandoned them to join the Black Panthers—won the Coretta Scott King Award and other honors. Its two follow-ups, *P.S. Be Eleven* and *Gone Crazy in Alabama*, keep the humor and period detail alive.

## The Thing About Luck

**Cynthia Kadohata**

Twelve-year-old Summer barely survives an attack of malaria, but at harvest time she still has to work in the Indiana fields with her Japanese American family, despite her fears of mosquitoes and feeling left behind when her parents suddenly have to leave for Japan. Charming and triumphantly positive.

## The Truth About Twinkie Pie

**Kat Yeh**

Two very different sisters. A culture-shock move from the trailer parks of South Carolina to the North Shore of Long Island. This novel about middle-school-age sisters, realistic and endearingly drawn, is full of heart.

## YA

### I'll Give You the Sun
**Jandy Nelson**

Boy and girl teenage twins, one of them gay, narrate alternate chapters of this exuberantly written, sad-happy novel about finding your true path and making a new life in the aftermath of tragedy.

### Far from the Tree
**Robin Benway**

The heroine of this lyrical novel is a pregnant teenager who has decided to give her baby up for adoption and was herself adopted. She says goodbye to her baby and tracks down her birth mother, finding siblings she never knew about. This book takes total possession of your heart.

### I Am Not Your Perfect Mexican Daughter
**Erika L. Sánchez**

Where does our obligation to our parents end—especially immigrant parents who have sacrificed so much? This affecting novel about a girl trying to outrun the shadow of her "perfect" but tragically dead sister is about navigating personal destiny alongside family bonds.

### Long Way Down
**Jason Reynolds**

Fifteen-year-old Will lives in a tough neighborhood, and when his beloved older brother is killed, he must decide if vengeance is the right response. This novel in verse goes right for the gut, then the heart.

### Hey, Kiddo
**Jarrett J. Krosoczka**

Raised by his grandparents because his mother couldn't break her drug habit, Krosoczka tells his childhood story with no holds barred, from the imperfect but loving grandparents who saved him to the art that became his lifeline. Best for ages 12 and up, it's brave and unforgettable.

## Great Friendship Stories

### PICTURE BOOKS

### Ten Things I Love About You
**Daniel Kirk**

A wonderful and too-rare story about boy friendship. This time, it's between a pig and a bunny. And there's no conflict! Simply the desire for each animal to show his appreciation of the other, through the shared task of writing down the qualities he most adores in his good friend. Pure sweetness.

### Alexander and the Wind-Up Mouse
**Leo Lionni**

Poor Alexander. Everyone loves Willy, the wind-up mouse, while he—a real mouse—is rejected and ignored. This Caldecott Honor book is about not only friendship but also appreciating differences and learning to love yourself for who you are.

## Duck & Goose
### Tad Hills
Interspecies friendship is possible, even for two feathered friends who don't always see eye to eye. The terrific original title—about a disagreement over an egg—has inspired enough spin-offs that there is one for practically any occasion or obstacle.

## Sophie's Squash
### Pat Zietlow Miller,
### illustrated by Anne Wilsdorf
Little Sophie forms a passionate attachment to a squash from the farmer's market. Children will root for her as she tries to bring her new friend everywhere; parents will admire the aplomb of the grown-ups as they help her transfer her affections to a flesh-and-blood friend. The follow-up, *Sophie's Squash Go to School*, is great, too.

## Jerome by Heart
### Thomas Scotto,
### illustrated by Olivier Tallec
A boy explains the passion he feels for his generous, funny, loyal friend Jerome in this refreshingly direct, winsome tribute to the strong bonds between boys.

## The Gift of Nothing
### Patrick McDonnell
Mooch the cat and Earl the dog, lifted from their Mutts comic strip, star in this minimalist tale that is about a lot more than the struggle to find the right present for a friend. The greatest gift of all, of course, is friendship.

## Baby Bear
### Kadir Nelson
This book about a lost bear looking for his way home with the help of his friends is also a story about finding your way in the world. Nelson's lush oil paintings have won him a Coretta Scott King Award and Caldecott Honor. The mesmerizing blues of night here show why.

## Big Wolf & Little Wolf
### Nadine Brun-Cosme,
### illustrated by Olivier Tallec
This charming French import (and its companion titles as well) tells the tale of two characters who come to friendship slowly, through the simple act of keeping each other company. Tallec's stunning landscapes and moody creatures elevate this sensitive book into a treasure.

## Friendshape
### Amy Krouse Rosenthal and
### Tom Lichtenheld
The dream team behind multiple books (*I Wish You More* and *Exclamation Mark*) use deceptively simple shapes, that differ on certain points, to tell a story about overcoming differences to find common ground.

## A Weekend with Wendell
### Kevin Henkes
Wendell is bossy and annoying. And worse, he's coming to spend the weekend at Sophie's house. Yes, they will find a way to actually get along.

## CHAPTER BOOKS AND MIDDLE GRADE

### Raymie Nightingale
**Kate DiCamillo**
When Raymie's dad leaves the family, she hatches a plan to persuade him to come back by entering and winning a baton-twirling contest. She'll be up against two girls from vastly different circumstances. In DiCamillo's expert telling, true friendship not only makes you laugh but also heals you. See also the equally appealing follow-up, *Louisiana's Way Home*, in which another of the girls takes the spotlight.

### Ava and Pip
**Carol Weston**
Ava and Pip are two sisters, one painfully shy and awkward, one outgoing. The gentle story and its two follow-ups, *Ava and Taco Cat* and *Ava XOX*, offer sneaky lessons in working through conflict and accommodating personality differences with kindness.

### The Lumberjanes series
**Noelle Stevenson, Grace Ellis, et al.**
Originally a webcomic, this series introduces a cast of quirky, adventuresome girlfriends who excel at wilderness survival as well as handling supernatural situations.

### The Wings of Fire series
**Tui T. Sutherland**
This high fantasy series about a world filled with dragons is (*shh*) also about friendship and relationships. The characters are richly drawn, and the dynamics among them often mirror the human world, full of nuance and very real emotion.

### The Cricket in Times Square
**George Selden**
This classic, set in a newspaper stand in the New York City subway, lets the friendship between a cat, a mouse, a cricket, and a boy unfold in an often heart-wrenching but deeply satisfying way.

### You Go First
**Erin Entrada Kelly**
Two middle schoolers going through personal struggles—a girl in Pennsylvania and a boy in Louisiana—forge a friendship playing online Scrabble, then meet in real life in a tale that explores the many ways to find honest connection with friends.

### The Lions of Little Rock
**Kristin Levine**
A white girl and a black girl become friends during the tumultuous integration of Little Rock's schools in the 1950s. A gripping and emotionally satisfying look at the unbreakable bonds of friendship.

### Posted
**John David Anderson**
When cell phones are banned at a middle school, kids start leaving sticky notes for each other—and it turns out the temptations to be cruel are just as strong. A clever, poignant look at the power of words to connect or to hurt.

### The Secret Tree
**Natalie Standiford**

A girl named Minty, facing troubles at home, discovers a tree in which the neighborhood kids leave notes telling their secrets. A lovely exploration of social bonds.

### The Baby-Sitters Club series
**Ann M. Martin**

Many women of a certain age grew up inhaling Ann M. Martin's series about a group of friends who start a babysitting business, learning as much about each other as they do about childcare. They've since been updated and turned into graphic novels in which a new generation of kids can see themselves and their peers. Once your kid is through all those, there's also *Best Babysitters Ever*, by Caroline Cala, a wickedly clever update in which current-day girls who've read the originals decide to start their own babysitting service, with raucous results.

## YA

### The Pigman
**Paul Zindel**

Written in the late 1960s, this story about two wiseacre teenagers who stumble into an unexpected friendship with an eccentric older stranger they're trying to prank still holds up. Few YA books feature this kind of cross-generational bond.

### The Outsiders
**S. E. Hinton**

Published in 1967 by the then 18-year-old Hinton, this classic is still vital, still winning kids over to the story of innocent Ponyboy and his loyal, hardscrabble gang, forced to defend themselves on the mean streets of Tulsa, Oklahoma.

### Dear Martin
**Nic Stone**

A present-day African American boy named Justyce writes letters addressed to Dr. Martin Luther King Jr., seeking guidance as he navigates police brutality toward black people and the complications of relationships with white classmates. Soaring and philosophical.

### I Will Always Write Back
**Caitlin Alifirenka and Martin Ganda, with Liz Welch**

This nonfiction account of the life-changing, enduring friendship between an American girl and an impoverished African boy who meet as pen pals for a school project takes your breath away. Perhaps only a true story could deliver this kind of emotional punch and encouragement.

### The Serpent King
**Jeff Zentner**

This novel about three misfit high school friends living in a rural Tennessee community where violence looms captures the intensity and selflessness of adolescent friendships. Zentner shows how friends can save kids whose parents can't help them rise above their circumstances.

# Fear and Bravery

## PICTURE BOOKS

### Brave Irene
**William Steig**
Irene Bobbin, the dressmaker's daughter, is selfless, dedicated, and determined. She sets off in a snowstorm to deliver a dress to the duchess, fierce and undeterred no matter how treacherous the obstacle. An endearing heroine to inspire all.

### The Lion & the Mouse
**Jerry Pinkney**
Pinkney has several masterful retellings of Aesop's fables, including "The Ant and the Grasshopper," but this one, with its artful, wordless story of the tale of the lion who spares a mouse and is repaid magnificently, delivers especially strong life wisdom and watercolor art you can't look away from.

### Jabari Jumps
**Gaia Cornwall**
The high board is so, so scary! But the squeeze of a father's hand, full of confidence and reassurance, can help. This compassionate and encouraging take on being scared focuses on learning to swim but applies to a lot more as well.

### Black Dog
**Levi Pinfold**
A lot of courage and a little bit of magic help a family that hides inside their house, afraid of a gigantic dog outside, until the littlest member confronts the beast and cajoles it into shrinking, making everyone realize there was nothing to fear.

### The Gruffalo
**Julia Donaldson,**
**illustrated by Axel Scheffler**
A massive sensation in the United Kingdom, this delightful rhyming tale follows a clever mouse through the forest as he avoids predators by conjuring up the imaginary threat of a terrible monster, the Gruffalo. But what if he's telling the truth?

### The Dark
**Lemony Snicket,**
**illustrated by Jon Klassen**
Does every child go through a period of nighttime fears? Even the few who don't will appreciate this forthright story about a boy making peace with the dark. By the author of A Series of Unfortunate Events and the illustrator of I Want My Hat Back, the writing and illustration here are both exquisite.

### Some Things Are Scary
**Florence Parry Heide,**
**illustrated by Jules Feiffer**
This hilarious and helpful account of familiar moments that nonetheless strike terror in our hearts—like skating downhill and not being able to stop— appeals to grown-ups just as much as kids.

### Ready to Ride
**Sébastien Pelon**
A boy is afraid to ride his bike without training wheels until a soft, amorphous white creature shows up to offer support, but only for as long as he truly needs it.

### After the Fall
**Dan Santat**
Of course you're supposed to get back on the horse again. But imagine if falling from a wall led to the total fracture and splat of your inner egg. Humpty Dumpty rises again in this ingenious book about bravely recuperating from defeat.

### There Are No Scary Wolves
**Hyewon Yum**
The world outside can be frightening, full of mysterious strangers and perhaps even wolves—even when you've got on your special cape. Yum's highly inventive drawings are more sweet than scary, charmingly evocative of a world in which the scariest things lie within our own imagination.

## CHAPTER BOOKS AND MIDDLE GRADE

### Hatchet
**Gary Paulsen**
This modern classic about a 13-year-old boy who survives a plane crash and spends days lost in the forest, finding food and making shelter with only a hatchet, has taught many a tween wilderness survival skills. There's also guidance on dealing with your parents' divorce.

### The Toys Go Out books
**Emily Jenkins,**
**illustrated by Paul O. Zelinsky**
In this funny, smart trio of chapter books, *Toys Go Out*, *Toys Come Home*, and *Toy Dance Party*, three friends—two stuffed animals and a rubber ball—navigate the scary world outside when the little girl who owns them leaves. Jenkins and Zelinsky also teamed up for a gorgeous wintertime picture book, perfect for introducing these lovable characters to younger children, called *Toys Meet Snow*.

### Umbrella Summer
**Lisa Graff**
Annie is a worrier, and her worst fear has actually been realized: Her brother has passed away. Grief stricken and terrified, she avoids taking any chances at all, until the summer, when she slowly learns to live with risk again.

### Turtle in Paradise
**Jennifer L. Holm**
Set during the Great Depression, this novel tells the story of an emotionally closed-off 10-year-old girl whose family loses everything and sends her to live with relatives in Florida, where she learns to build trust and a new life.

### The Breadwinner
**Deborah Ellis**
Ellis interviewed young Afghan refugees before writing this fictional story of a girl who musters her courage to go out dressed as a boy to earn money for her family. There's a compelling graphic novel, too.

## Stella by Starlight
**Sharon M. Draper**
Set in the Jim Crow South, this suspenseful story centers on a black girl who faces up to the menace of the Ku Klux Klan to save her mother after a snakebite. Resounds with courage and a celebration of community.

## Cartwheeling in Thunderstorms
**Katherine Rundell**
An orphan story, a boarding-school story, a fish-out-of-water story, and more. A white girl living in Africa is sent to an English boarding school after her father dies, forging a courageous new life there.

## Where the Mountain Meets the Moon
**Grace Lin**
Lin weaves together legends from Chinese mythology and timeless adventure stories in these tales, stunningly illustrated in full color. Together with two subsequent companion novels, these books are filled with magical creatures and brave children determined to fulfill their destinies.

## The Epic Fail of Arturo Zamora
**Pablo Cartaya**
A baseball-playing boy in Miami schemes against a sinister real-estate developer who threatens to take over his grandma's restaurant. A funny, touching novel about finding the power to stand up for what matters.

## Orphan Island
**Laurel Snyder**
Nine orphans live on a mysterious island with no adults, but every year the oldest is taken away and replaced—until a girl named Jinny decides she's not sure she wants to go along when her time comes. Enchanting and thought provoking, with wonderful layers of symbolism.

# YA

## Challenger Deep
**Neal Shusterman**
This account of a teenage boy's battle with schizophrenia is riveting and informative about living with mental illness. There's heart and courage to spare on every page.

## Turtles All the Way Down
**John Green**
Many teenagers suffer from anxiety, and this novel about a girl crippled by her obsessive thoughts—who nonetheless solves a mystery and falls in love—is all the more riveting and important for being based on Green's own struggles with mental illness.

## If I Stay
**Gayle Forman**
A teenager, in the midst of deciding whether to leave home and her boyfriend to pursue music, is left in a coma by a car accident. Forman glides back and forth in time to paint a heartbreaking picture of a teen facing a true crisis that puts her whole life in perspective.

## Highly Illogical Behavior
**John Corey Whaley**
Whaley brings his trademark wacky humor and big heart to this story of a teenage boy with agoraphobia who's terrified of leaving the house, and the misguided friend who tries to help him.

## American Street
**Ibi Zoboi**
Fabiola is en route to Detroit from an earthquake-ravaged Haiti to live with her cousins when her mother is detained by immigration authorities, leaving her to navigate a new country, language, and family alone. Beguiling, with just a sprinkle of magical realism.

## Yaqui Delgado Wants to Kick Your Ass
**Meg Medina**
There aren't enough stories out there about girl bullies, but this one shines brightly: A brainy Latina girl, deemed "too white," is harassed by other girls. She learns to stand up for herself without shutting down her sensitivity, while also dealing with family issues and a part-time job at a hair salon.

## A Monster Calls
**Patrick Ness,**
**illustrated by Jim Kay**
Based on a novel by the late Siobhan Dowd, this big-hearted book finds unexpected ways to tackle the subject of a boy learning to deal with his mother's death. There's also a well-regarded movie version.

## Divergent trilogy
**Veronica Roth**
One of the most addictive of the apocalyptic teen-competition sagas, this series lays out a world in which kids are forcibly grouped into one of five oppressive factions at the age of 16. It takes courage and more for the heroine to find a path that lets her be true to herself.

## We All Looked Up
**Tommy Wallach**
What would you do if you knew an asteroid would hit the earth in three months, wiping everything out? Four teenagers in Seattle face a terrifying, ultimate endgame. As philosophical as it is unsettling.

## Blood Water Paint
**Joy McCullough**
Based on the life of the Italian baroque painter Artemisia Gentileschi, who found the courage to press charges against her rapist, this breathtaking novel in prose and verse digs deep to tell an age-old story about standing up for yourself even in the face of injustice and violence.

# Kindness and Empathy

## PICTURE BOOKS

### I Am Human

Susan Verde,
illustrated by Peter H. Reynolds

A little boy traipses delightfully through these pages, proclaiming all that makes him—and all of us—human, from making honest mistakes to reaching out in kindness to others.

### The Three Robbers

Tomi Ungerer

With Ungerer's signature humor and sly language, three marauding robbers take in an innocent child, Tiffany. With kindness and an open belief in human goodness, she creates Robin Hoods out of their greed. A treasure for all.

### The Giving Tree

Shel Silverstein

This book is a polarizing one, with many parents persuaded that it illustrates the perils of the selfless mother. But others (including us) see it as a more nuanced moral tale about the occasionally blurry lines between generosity and selfishness, and the complex nature of relationships. At what point can being "giving" mean giving too much of yourself away? Whichever way you view the book personally, it will be sure to provoke conversation and debate with your child. Also, it's a beautiful story about a boy growing up.

### I Walk with Vanessa: A Story About a Simple Act of Kindness

Kerascoët

Bullying can happen even among very young children. This deceptively simple but powerful wordless tale, inspired by a true story, shows how one child's actions can inspire an entire community.

### Most People

Michael Leannah,
illustrated by Jennifer E. Morris

The world out there can be alarming, with even young children bombarded by images of war, brutality, gun violence, dying children, and hate speech. Created as a helpful antidote to those omnipresent threats, this book carries simple message: Most people are good. Respond to and connect with others. Appreciate our common humanity, and don't lose faith in the power of goodness.

### Why Am I Me?

Paige Britt,
illustrated by Sean Qualls and Selina Alko

Two parent-and-child pairs of different races encounter one another while traveling by subway. This poetic meditation on identity and differences addresses children's most basic questions about what makes people different yet also alike.

### Courage

**Bernard Waber**

Every one of us is capable of great brav-
ery, whether faced with threats large or
small: tasting a new vegetable, facing
a scary dog, or taking off your training
wheels. Waber shows how helping each
other overcome the fears we all share
helps bind a community.

### The Smallest Girl in the Smallest Grade

**Justin Roberts,**
**illustrated by Christian Robinson**

This book, perfect for younger children, tells the story of Sally McCabe,
a small child whom nobody notices
but who notices everything. When she
sees bullying in the playground, she is
big enough to stand up to it. Christian
Robinson is one of the most talented
illustrators working today, as these
tender images show.

### Not So Different: What You Really Want to Ask About Having a Disability

**Shane Burcaw**

A frank, first-person account by
someone with a rare disease, spinal
muscular atrophy, which causes his
body to weaken and grow smaller as he
gets older. He answers, with frankness
and humor, all of those uncomfortable
questions that curious children want to
know: "How do you play with friends?"
"What's wrong with you?"

### Mallko and Dad

**Gusti**

This tender look at the day-to-day life
of a boy with Down syndrome and his
dad, who was at first upset to learn of
his son's condition, explodes with heart,
courage, and humor. A beautiful, necessary book for all ages.

### This Is How We Do It: One Day in the Lives of Seven Kids from Around the World

**Matt Lamothe**

Children from countries around the
world, from Iran to Peru, describe their
everyday activities in this beautifully
illustrated look at the way kids live now.
A global guide infused with lessons
about geography, culture, and history.

### Be a Friend

**Salina Yoon**

Dennis, a boy who prefers to mime
rather than speak, forges a friendship
with a girl named Joy. Is he unable to
speak? Is he scared to? Is he autistic? It
doesn't matter; Joy accepts him. Yoon's
gentle story and illustrations are a celebration of the wonders of connection.

### The Journey

**Francesca Sanna**

This debut story about a family of
migrants fleeing an unspecified war
won a suite of awards for its sensitive,
age-appropriate treatment of a difficult
subject. Children have questions about
the headlines they absorb; this book
offers answers.

### My Beautiful Birds
**Suzanne Del Rizzo**
A Syrian boy mourns the beloved pigeons he must leave behind in fleeing to Lebanon but finds new birds to care for at a refugee camp. For slightly older picture book readers, this story humanizes the Syrian refugee crisis with artful mixed media.

### Last Stop on Market Street
**Matt de la Peña,**
**illustrated by Christian Robinson**
A little boy named CJ rides the bus with his nana, complaining all the way, but she makes him see the positive side of every annoyance—and when they arrive at their destination, a soup kitchen where they're volunteering, your heart will be full.

### Be Kind
**Pat Zietlow Miller,**
**illustrated by Jen Hill**
It's so simple and so necessary to fill your life with thoughtful, generous acts, and this lovely book shows the youngest children how to do that, without preaching.

### Zen Ties, Zen Shorts, AND Zen Ghosts
**Jon J Muth**
Illustrated in serene watercolors, these simple, hypnotic books incorporate haiku as well as basic concepts of Zen philosophy, such as patience and moderation, through stories about three siblings and a giant panda named Stillwater.

### Rude Cakes
**Rowboat Watkins**
Starring a family of cakes, this may be the funniest and least preachy book about manners you will read to your child. Kindness begins with basic manners, after all. Humor doesn't hurt.

### Herman the Helper
**Robert Kraus,**
**illustrated by Jose Aruego and**
**Ariane Dewey**
Herman is a tiny little octopus who helps other sea creatures just because. And everyone appreciates it! Yet there's nothing didactic about the sheer adorableness of this happy little tale.

### Come with Me
**Holly M. McGhee,**
**illustrated by Pascal Lemaître**
Faced with the fear and hatred she observes on the nightly TV news, a young girl asks her father what she can do to help. "Come with me," he says, offering a powerful message about the importance of spreading kindness, even in small ways, even in tough times.

## CHAPTER BOOKS AND MIDDLE GRADE

### Bigger Than a Bread Box
**Laurel Snyder**
Being made a pawn in her parents' angry separation, as well as being forced to move to a new home in another state, is stressful for 12-year-old Rebecca. A magical bread box seems to offer an easy way to solve her problems. Snyder delivers a nuanced exploration of facing difficulty with grace and understanding.

### Mockingbird
**Kathryn Erksine**
Things seem bleak when a girl with Asperger's syndrome loses her brother in a school shooting, but a strong community and unbounded kindness help these poignant characters navigate the rockiest of life's roads.

### Refugee
**Alan Gratz**
Three suspenseful and linked stories in this volume—about kids who are refugees in Nazi Germany and contemporary Cuba and Syria—shine a light on the plight of refugees and the connections between all of us.

### Maniac Magee
**Jerry Spinelli**
A freak accident makes the hero of this wise and funny book an orphan. But after years of "acting out," he finds a better path, becoming the unifier of a racially divided small town.

### Merci Suárez Changes Gears
**Meg Medina**
This warm and funny Newbery Medal winner is about a Florida girl who lives with her Cuban American extended family and must find a way to be herself, gracefully, in the face of confusing new demands, including her grandfather's descent into Alzheimer's and shifts in the social dynamics at her private school, where she's a scholarship student.

### A Long Walk to Water
**Linda Sue Park**
Two kids in Sudan, one in 1985 and one in 2008, navigate extreme hardship to create a better future for themselves. This internationally recognized book has raised awareness of the heroic feats children can achieve.

### Hello, Universe
**Erin Entrada Kelly**
One bully, three unlikely friends, and a world of insight into building empathic relationships. This recent Newbery Medal winner sneaks into your heart, making you think everyone can learn to grow compassion.

### Gone-Away Lake
**Elizabeth Enright**
In this mid-twentieth-century classic, two children discover a ghostly lakeside resort that needs to be sparked back to life, requiring hard work and an understanding of others they didn't know they were capable of.

## The Witches of Worm
### Zilpha Keatley Snyder

This slim, unforgettable classic is creepy and downright scary at times, forcing a reckoning with the question: What bad stuff would I be capable of under certain circumstances? A neglected girl named Jessica takes in a sickly, bewitched kitten who leads her to commit mischief and worse—or is it her own frustration and anger causing her to take a dark turn?

## A Little Princess
### Frances Hodgson Burnett

This book was published more than one hundred years ago, but the story is as affecting as ever. Young Sara, sent to an English boarding school by her army captain father stationed in India, goes from riches to rags and back to riches again as she learns generosity and patience, and develops an understanding of all walks of life.

# YA

## Love and First Sight
### Josh Sundquist

A boy blind from birth starts high school, learning to find his own way and developing a crush on a sighted girl. When a new surgery offers him the chance to see, everything must be reevaluated. Deeply thought provoking.

## The Skin I'm In
### Sharon G. Flake

A dark-skinned African American girl who's used to being teased about her looks and her poverty turns a corner toward self-acceptance when a new teacher arrives who has both a startling skin condition and an infectiously positive attitude. Inspiring and affirming.

## A Step Toward Falling
### Cammie McGovern

After a teenage girl with a developmental disability is viciously attacked at a high school, two kids who were bystanders must do community service and are transformed in the process. McGovern gently defuses prejudice by depicting the full lives of those with intellectual disabilities.

## The 57 Bus
### Dashka Slater

A beautifully written nonfiction account of an incident in which a teenager was set on fire by another on a Bay Area bus. There are no easy answers; there's just an invitation to social awareness and compassion for both the victim and the attacker.

## A Land of Permanent Goodbyes
### Atia Abawi

A Syrian boy named Tareq lives comfortably with his big, loving family until the war sends them fleeing as refugees. A harrowing tale of the consequences of war and the resilience of a hopeful teenager.

## The Distance Between Us: Young Reader's Edition
### Reyna Grande

This award-winning memoir recounts Grande's childhood journey to the United States from her native Mexico to join her difficult father, an undocumented immigrant. Full of great writing as well as heartbreak, hope, and hard truths.

### How Dare the Sun Rise: Memoirs of a War Child
**Sandra Uwiringiyimana, with Abigail Pesta**
An eloquent narrative of a girl's traumatic journey from Africa and her struggle to make a new life in the United States. Every page reminds us that the word *refugee* is woefully inadequate to encompass a life.

### Soldier Boy
**Keely Hutton**
Mixing fiction with nonfiction, this story of the boys forced to fight in Joseph Kony's army in Uganda is shocking and eye-opening. Includes an inspirational look inside an organization working to save and rehabilitate child soldiers.

### The Librarian of Auschwitz
**Antonio Iturbe**
Based on a true story, this novel presents a 14-year-old prisoner at Auschwitz who risked her life to protect precious books her fellow Jews had smuggled in. Searing and sophisticated.

### Love, Hate & Other Filters
**Samira Ahmed**
An American-born Muslim teenager who wants to study film grapples with Islamophobia and her protective parents. An absorbing story of reaching across cultural and religious fault lines.

# Self-Acceptance and Identity

## PICTURE BOOKS

### Leo the Late Bloomer
**Robert Krauss, illustrated by Jose Aruego**
A small tiger fears he is no good at anything and not nearly advanced as his peers but is reassured that his talents, skills, and strengths will show through eventually. For some tigers, it just takes time.

### Swimmy
**Leo Lionni**
There's good reason this charming book about a brave little minnow who leads his fellow fish from danger endures (and it's the perfect antidote to *The Rainbow Fish*, which champions conformity). Good leadership doesn't require great size, and the best leaders know about teamwork.

### Exclamation Mark
**Amy Krouse Rosenthal, illustrated by Tom Lichtenheld**
This paean to self-acceptance weaves humor into its deceptively simple and adorable illustrations about a punctuation mark that just doesn't fit in.

## Chrysanthemum
**Kevin Henkes**

It's hard to get to school loving your name, only to discover that everyone else finds it ridiculous. A heartwarming tale of resilience about a mouse who is teased about her name, from the ever-astonishing Henkes.

## The Caboose Who Got Loose
**Bill Peet**

Peet, an animator on many of the early Disney classics and a prolific author-illustrator whose works are still largely available in paperback, specializes in misfit characters and misunderstandings. Impossible dreams, too. In this story, Katy doesn't like being the last car on the train, and she describes precisely why in charmingly rhymed couplets before discovering that being the last one doesn't always end badly. Peet's other hits include *Pamela Camel, How Droofus the Dragon Lost His Head,* and *The Whingdingdilly.*

## Julián Is a Mermaid
**Jessica Love**

The famed Coney Island Mermaid Parade is captured in a story about a boy who sees a bevy of costumed mermaids on the subway one afternoon while riding with his *abuela.* And why can't a boy be a mermaid, too? Luminous.

## The Story of Ferdinand
**Munro Leaf,**
**illustrated by Robert Lawson**

Is this beloved classic an antiwar parable? Perhaps, but the story of a peaceful bull who just longs to sit under a cork tree and smell the flowers needn't be read on a political level at all. Children will appreciate the simple story of an animal comfortable in his own skin.

## Stellaluna
**Janell Cannon**

A baby fruit bat is knocked from his family nest by an attacking owl, forcing him to take up with a set of unfamiliar birds. This modern classic is about the balancing act of accommodating others while staying true to who you really are. Bats have never looked quite so pretty.

## The Invisible Boy
**Trudy Ludwig,**
**illustrated by Patrice Barton**

The other kids are noisy. Nobody picks him for the kickball team. Brian feels completely invisible until a new boy, Justin, comes to school and finally notices him. Barton's pastels perfectly match this story about seeing the shy children in our midst and recognizing their worth.

## John Jensen Feels Different
**Henrik Hovland,**
**illustrated by Torill Kove**

Is it his tail? His bow tie? Why does John J. Jensen feel so very different from everyone else in his northern European town? This classic learn-to-love-who-you-are story is distinguished by its droll humor and appealing Norwegian aesthetic.

## Chapter Books and Middle Grade

### Rain Reign
**Ann M. Martin**
A girl with autism faces giving up the rescue dog she's bonded with when she discovers its original owners. This heartwarming book by the beloved author of The Baby-Sitters Club series sheds important light on what it's like to be—or to get to know—someone on the autism spectrum.

### Out of My Mind
**Sharon M. Draper**
A girl who uses a wheelchair because of cerebral palsy enters a traditional classroom where she is at first bullied, until her classmates learn a deep lesson about the power of friendship. This novel stealthily opens hearts and minds to the experiences of kids with disabilities.

### Amal Unbound
**Aisha Saeed**
A 12-year-old Pakistani girl who dreams of being a teacher is forced to work for a rich family and becomes increasingly aware of their criminality. A moving look at what it takes to hold on to your identity in challenging circumstances.

### Wonderstruck
**Brian Selznick**
Brian Selznick's trademark hybrid storytelling—pages of only illustration and pages of only words—is especially well suited to this brilliant tale of a deaf girl seeking her estranged mother and a fatherless boy who loses his ability to speak after a lightning storm. Selznick conveys a connection that goes far beyond words.

### See You in the Cosmos
**Jack Cheng**
A lonely boy obsessed with space and the astronomer Carl Sagan, and whose single mom is not very functional, is out to launch his iPod into space in this tenderhearted novel that gently probes big questions about the universe and a family's place in it.

### The Great Gilly Hopkins
**Katherine Paterson**
This modern classic about a girl who's brash and "unmanageable" after years shuttling between foster homes is a great exploration of children's anger and sense of unfairness, and it shows how even a troubled kid can find a path to hope and change.

### All's Faire in Middle School
**Victoria Jamieson**
When you've grown up being homeschooled at a Renaissance faire, it's not easy to fit in at middle school. This gem of a graphic novel sneakily shows the many faces bullying and unkindness can wear, and how they can be vanquished.

### The Way to Bea
**Kat Yeh**
A seventh grader who feels like an utter outsider writes haiku in invisible ink. When someone starts writing back, she forms a new friendship with a kid obsessed with labyrinths. A frank but

sensitive look at both the cruelty of middle school and the value of being a little bit quirky.

## The Boy Called Bat series
**Elana K. Arnold,**
**illustrated by Charles Santoso**
Bixby Alexander Tam, nicknamed Bat, is on the autism spectrum. These funny, sweet books do a stellar job of showing what's different—and what's the same—for kids who are not neurotypical.

## Ivy Aberdeen's Letter to the World
**Ashley Herring Blake**
Eleven-year-old Ivy has not only lost her home in a tornado but is trying to figure out her feelings for her best friend. This is the rare middle-grade novel that deals with same-sex attraction, and it does so gently and wisely.

## YA

## The Poet X
**Elizabeth Acevedo**
A Dominican girl in New York City finds her voice as a slam poet in this electrifying novel in verse by acclaimed slam poet Acevedo. A tribute to the power of words and a sensitive exploration of family, ethnic, and religious identity.

## Dumplin'
**Julie Murphy**
A self-proclaimed "fat girl" with a beauty-queen mom is just starting to feel confident when she decides to enter a beauty contest and make a statement. Murphy uses a strong, warm voice to address the pressures of body image on teenage girls.

## We Are Okay
**Nina LaCour**
This hauntingly beautiful, Printz Award–winning novel is about a girl facing the bewilderment and paralysis of grief. It also depicts young lesbian love with tenderness and grace.

## Wintergirls
**Laurie Halse Anderson**
No one handles dark teenage realities better than Anderson, and this is one of her most powerful stories: Two friends suffer from eating disorders, one fatally; the survivor must find the courage to go on and stay healthy.

## The Uglies series
**Scott Westerfeld**
The toxic culture of body-image obsession gets a dystopian spin in this series about a society where 16-year-olds are forced to undergo surgery to make them "pretties," but some girls rebel and demand the right to think for themselves.

## The List
**Siobhan Vivian**
Set in a high school where a list appears every year naming the prettiest and the ugliest girl, this brisk, insightful novel shows the difficult but worthwhile path toward true self-esteem in a status-obsessed environment.

### American Born Chinese
**Gene Luen Yang**
A Monkey King from Chinese mythology, a bit of martial arts, and the perilous American middle-school social landscape combine seamlessly in this story of Chinese American boys finding their own inner superheroes.

### The Great American Whatever
**Tim Federle**
A gay teenage boy whose older sister has just died in a car wreck faces the hurdles of constructing a new life without her, as well as navigating his first romance. Funny and true: The heartbreak glides by between smiles and laughs.

### Every Day
**David Levithan**
This unique and captivating book explores the pressures of gender identity through the story of a boy who wakes up every day in a different body. A mind-bender that hits teens right in their philosophical sweet spot.

### The Tightrope Walkers
**David Almond**
Set in northern England during the 1950s and '60s, this book chronicles a working-class teenage boy's journey toward adulthood. A realistic, extraordinarily compassionate look at the difficulty of navigating masculinity, violence, creativity, and identity.

## Great Boy Characters

### PICTURE BOOKS

### Draw! AND Imagine!
**Raúl Colón**
These gorgeous wordless stories show an artistic young boy's journey toward embracing and following his penchant for drawing and his prodigious imagination.

### Yo! Yes
**Chris Raschka**
Two boys, one black and one white, meet and decide to try being friends. The book's few words and expressive images capture something deep and exciting in the boys' embrace of a new possibility.

### Sam and the Tigers
**Julius Lester,**
**illustrated by Jerry Pinkney**
This book about a boy who outwits a pack of tigers is an exhilaratingly clever celebration of gutsiness and braininess—and all the better because, although modern kids won't know this, it's actually a retelling of the classically racist story "Little Black Sambo," with a smart black kid as the hero.

### Lentil
**Robert McCloskey**
This classic from the author of *Make Way for Ducklings* introduces a boy who'd like to be a singer but finds that his true talent is playing harmonica,

culminating in the chance to play in a parade through town.

### The Raft
**Jim LaMarche**
Nicky is sullen about being stuck at Grandma's for the summer but discovers the satisfactions of fishing and rafting on the river, as well as his grandmother's rural wisdom. LaMarche's stunning, painterly illustrations capture the joy of a child happily immersed in nature.

## CHAPTER BOOKS AND MIDDLE GRADE

### The Witch Boy
**Molly Knox Ostertag**
Girls are witches, boys are shapeshifters. That's just the way it is. Set in a socially rigid magical land, this graphic novel tells how 13-year-old Aster manages to find his own way as a nonconforming but nonetheless powerful witch.

### The Waylon! books
**Sara Pennypacker**
Fourth grader Waylon likes science and inventing things, but he also has to attend to various explosions in his friend group and his family. A spin-off from the author's Clementine books.

### All Rise for the Honorable Perry T. Cook
**Leslie Connor**
Eleven-year-old Perry was born and raised in a Nebraska correctional facility where his mom is doing time, but when a new warden forces him to move to foster care, Perry has to draw on an untapped well of resilience. Warm and full of hope and forgiveness.

### Better Nate Than Ever
**Tim Federle**
Theater kids will find themselves in this funny, insightful tale of a young thespian who dreams of Broadway. It's hard not to be drawn in by Nate's touching awkwardness and drive to follow his heart and find his true destiny no matter what. The follow-ups, *Five, Six, Seven, Nate!* and *Nate Expectations* deliver, as well.

### The Invention of Hugo Cabret
**Brian Selznick**
A visually sumptuous mystery about an orphan who lives secretly in the walls of a Paris train station, keeping the clock. Suspense and unexpected emotion build as you turn the pages rapturously.

## YA

### Dear Evan Hansen: The Novel
**Val Emmich**
The novelization of the Tony Award–winning Broadway show feels inevitable, and it works. Evan Hansen is a boy without friends who finds himself, loses himself, then finds himself again through the fateful suicide of another loner.

### The Prince and the Dressmaker
**Jen Wang**
This gender-bending, stereotype-skewering graphic novel features a prince who enjoys cross-dressing and his friendship with a female dressmaker. The illustrations are suitably sumptuous.

### All American Boys
**Jason Reynolds and Brendan Kiely**
This riveting novel by two of the greats of current YA is narrated in alternating chapters by two average boys, one African American and one white, who grapple honestly with an incident of race-based police brutality.

### Darius the Great Is Not Okay
**Adib Khorram**
A half-Persian, self-described Star Trek nerd with father *and* body-image issues reluctantly travels to Iran to visit family and learns about friendship—and himself—in this tender, funny novel.

### Too Shattered for Mending
**Peter Brown Hoffmeister**
This gorgeously written novel is about a sensitive, six-foot-five high school sophomore with dyslexia, who lives in a rough, drug-ravaged Idaho town. Abandoned by his grandfather and charged with caring for a young cousin, he learns to take care of himself, too, in the face of the toxic masculinity that surrounds him.

# Great Girl Characters

## PICTURE BOOKS

### A Gold Star for Zog
**Julia Donaldson,**
**illustrated by Axel Scheffler**
Told in clever rhyme, this story about young dragons learning their trade (roaring, breathing fire, and more) at dragon school is notable for its princess who refuses to play a damsel in distress or be rescued. What she wants is to become a doctor.

### This Is Sadie
**Sara O'Leary,**
**illustrated by Julie Morstad**
Sadie is an imaginative little girl who dreams she can do anything: She can fly. She can tell stories. She can make things, like boats out of boxes and castles out of cushions. She's a dreamer *and* a doer.

### Drum Dream Girl: How One Girl's Courage Changed Music
**Margarita Engle,**
**illustrated by Rafael López**
In Cuba, girls aren't meant to drum. But don't tell that to the drum dream girl, a character inspired by the real-life figure Millo Castro Zaldarriaga, a Chinese African Cuban girl who pursued drumming despite cultural taboos.

### Young Charlotte, Filmmaker
**Frank Viva**
The celebrated *New Yorker* artist and picture book author tells the story of a girl who wants to make black-and-white movies. When she meets Scarlet, a film curator at the Museum of Modern Art, she finds opportunity. A book about artistic vision, sticking to your guns, and the love of cats.

### Extra Yarn
**Mac Barnett,**
**illustrated by Jon Klassen**
A girl brings color to a monotone town with the help of special yarn in this magical modern fairy tale. She also manages to thwart an evil archduke. Quirky and infused with humor. A great companion to this one is *The Odious Ogre* by Norton Juster, with Jules Feiffer illustrating, in which another plucky heroine outwits a brute.

## CHAPTER BOOKS AND MIDDLE GRADE

### The Princeless books
**Jeremy Whitley**
These action-packed graphic novels do a particularly good job of defusing stereotypical passive, beauty- and boy-obsessed princess myths, with a dark-skinned princess who hates her royal status and takes matters into her own capable hands.

### The Mad Wolf's Daughter
**Diane Magras**
Set in medieval Scotland, this novel sends its smart, feisty young heroine through forests, towns, and many perils to save her father and brothers from the clutches of kidnappers, reminding us that female ingenuity can make independence possible in all kinds of settings.

### Are You There God? It's Me, Margaret.
**Judy Blume**
It's possible that no female character in all of literature has influenced as many lives as Margaret Simon, who has helped countless girls deal with the excitement and confusion of their first period. Sure, times have changed (*belts*?), but we'd wager Margaret's story will live forever.

### Harriet the Spy
**Louise Fitzhugh**
What more can we say about the great Harriet? The iconic, notebook-keeping heroine's story is still a must-read for curious, independent-minded kids and budding writers.

### Julie of the Wolves
**Jean Craighead George**
Kids (and adults) who love nature and adventure stories will thrill to this classic story of an Inuit girl who ends up lost in the Arctic wild and survives by learning to live and communicate with a pack of wolves. Julie is one of the truly unforgettable heroines of kidlit.

## YA

### Eleanor & Park
**Rainbow Rowell**
This bestseller pairs a tomboyish redheaded girl with a half-Korean, half-Vietnamese boy whose preference for comic books and penchant for wearing makeup puts him at odds with his sporty family. Set in the nineties (there are mixtapes), this appealing love story celebrates connections between kids who otherwise feel set apart.

### Friends with Boys
**Faith Erin Hicks**
Maggie grows up homeschooled and surrounded by older brothers. Then she has to face public school and its attendant social anxieties. Based on a webcomic, this graphic novel features bold black-and-white art—and a ghost.

### Anya's Ghost
**Vera Brosgol**
Another standout graphic novel featuring a teenage girl and a ghost. Self-conscious, perpetually embarrassed, and feeling like an outsider as a Russian immigrant, Anya initially welcomes the company of a seemingly friendly ghost. But said ghost may not be altogether friendly.

### I Am Still Alive
**Kate Alice Marshall**
This thriller will have you turning pages furiously as its teenage heroine finds herself stranded alone with a dog in the Canadian wilderness, digging deep to find the strength and smarts to fend off menaces that include the thugs whom she knows killed her dad.

### This One Summer
**Jillian Tamaki and Mariko Tamaki**
The rare graphic novel to win a Caldecott Honor, this emotionally sophisticated, teen-appropriate story takes place over one of those life-changing summers. An introspective heroine goes to her family's usual summer retreat, but everything is different, from her parents' fighting to dangerous behavior by the local teens.

# History and Biography

## PICTURE BOOKS

### The Boy Who Loved Math: The Improbable Life of Paul Erdös
**Deborah Heiligman,
illustrated by LeUyen Pham**
This picture book biography of the famous mathematician will appeal to young children who may have trouble concentrating on school, and equal trouble imagining a life of intellectual greatness ahead. This book shows that genius comes in many forms and isn't always evident to teachers and other grown-ups early on.

### Frederick Douglass: The Lion Who Wrote History
**Walter Dean Myers,
illustrated by Floyd Cooper**
This elegantly written and illustrated picture book biography introduces younger children to Douglass, and to the history of slavery, by focusing on how he pursued reading and learning to fight his and others' enslavement.

## Freedom in Congo Square
**Carole Boston Weatherford,
illustrated by R. Gregory Christie**
In Louisiana, slaves toiled all week in anticipation of a half day of freedom in New Orleans's Congo Square, where every Sunday they were at liberty to play music, dance, sing, and eat together. This poetic multiple-award winner recounts that celebration.

## I Have a Dream
**Dr. Martin Luther King Jr.,
illustrated by Kadir Nelson**
Nelson, whose uniformly excellent children's books often are filled with lush oil paintings, chose to accompany the words to King's famous speech with a simpler illustrative line. But his soaring, majestic paintings match the tenor of those inspiring words.

## The Boy Who Harnessed the Wind: Creating Currents of Electricity and Hope
**William Kamkwamba and Bryan Mealer,
illustrated by Elizabeth Zunon**
This is the picture book version of a bestselling memoir by Kamkwamba, who at age 14 figured out how to harness energy through a windmill and bring power to his impoverished Malawi village. Also recommended: *Energy Island* by Allan Drummond, about a community rallying together to bring wind power to the Danish island of Samso.

## Shackleton's Journey
**William Grill**
An oversized wonder of a nonfiction picture book, ideal for ages 7 and up. The life and accomplishments of the legendary Antarctic explorer, told narratively and through evocative illustrations, maps, and charts.

## Radiant Child: The Story of Young Artist Jean-Michel Basquiat
**Javaka Steptoe**
Steptoe's Caldecott-winning artwork reflects the style and energy of Basquiat himself as he recounts the early years and rise to fame of the Haitian–Puerto Rican artist. More standout artist bios: *Cloth Lullaby: The Woven Life of Louise Bourgeois* by Amy Novesky, illustrated by Isabelle Arsenault; *The Wall: Growing Up Behind the Iron Curtain* by Peter Sís; *Frida* by Jonah Winter, illustrated by Ana Juan; *The Fantastic Jungles of Henri Rousseau* by Michelle Markel, illustrated by Amanda Hall; and *Boys of Steel: The Creators of Superman* by Marc Tyler Nobleman, illustrated by Ross MacDonald.

## The Man Who Walked Between the Towers
**Mordicai Gerstein**
This is the Caldecott-winning tale of when Philippe Petit walked a wire between the Twin Towers of the World Trade Center. Petit's derring-do will capture the imaginations of children and adults alike. Check out another Gerstein great, *I Am Pan!*, about the wild and wonderful Greek god.

### Ruth Bader Ginsburg: The Case of R. B. G. vs. Inequality
**Jonah Winter,
illustrated by Stacy Innerst**
There are now a striking number of picture book biographies of Justice Ruth Bader Ginsburg; this one has a strong narrative focus and art that stands out from the pack. The prolific Winter knows how to get age-appropriate nonfiction just right.

### Helen's Big World: The Life of Helen Keller
**Doreen Rappaport,
illustrated by Matt Tavares**
There are many great books about Helen Keller, but this one's large, awe-inspiring, close-up artwork and powerful emotional punch make it top-notch. Each book in the Big Words series takes care to weave its subject's own words throughout the text, gracefully done here.

## CHAPTER BOOKS AND MIDDLE GRADE

### Titanic: Voices from the Disaster
**Deborah Hopkinson**
A jillion children's books address the disaster. This one, by the talented Hopkinson, makes use of witness and survivor narrators' accounts to enliven the story and enhance the action. The perfect bridge to history for kids who love thrillers.

### Bomb: The Race to Build—and Steal—the World's Most Dangerous Weapon
**Steve Sheinkin**
Perhaps Sheinkin's very best, this riveting account of the international race to build the atomic bomb will grip kids interested in the military, war, history, and science—and probably wrangle in kids *not* interested in those topics as well. Masterful narrative nonfiction storytelling.

### Amelia Lost: The Life and Disappearance of Amelia Earhart
**Candace Fleming**
Readers are eternally drawn to the beautiful and brave Earhart and her tragic end. Everything Fleming writes is superb, and this volume, immaculately researched, well balanced (Earhart had her flaws), and handsomely illustrated throughout, is *the* one you want on the pioneering aviatrix.

### Lincoln: A Photobiography
**Russell Freedman**
Freedman pioneered this photo-heavy way of writing history for young people, and this Newbery Medal winner offers an astonishing, full picture of Lincoln the man. This lively book is a school staple, but don't let that turn you off. A few more Lincoln bios worthy of the list: *Looking at Lincoln* by Maira Kalman and *Abe Lincoln Crosses a Creek* by Deborah Hopkinson and John Hendrix.

### The Plot to Kill Hitler: Dietrich Bonhoeffer: Pastor, Spy, Unlikely Hero
**Patricia McCormick**

This meticulously researched book sacrifices neither factual accuracy nor storytelling; it's a true page-turner. The story of a privileged young minister's decision to take a stand against the Nazis' evil is humbling and inspiring. Kids love stories of people who rise up against the bullies of the world. To that end, we also love *The Boys Who Challenged Hitler* by Phillip Hoose.

### Undefeated: Jim Thorpe and the Carlisle Indian School Football Team
**Steve Sheinkin**

What's not to like about a great under-dog sports story? Especially one that highlights an overlooked achievement of our Native American population—inventing the modern game of football—and the grave injustices they bore along the way. Sheinkin has won every award for nonfiction children's book writing; here's why.

### The Borden Murders: Lizzie Borden & the Trial of the Century
**Sarah Miller**

"Lizzie Borden took an axe, gave her mother forty whacks . . ." That twisted rhyme has haunted generations of Americans and, not surprisingly, intrigues young readers. This true-crime account is the best one for young readers on the "murder of the century."

### Survivors Club: The True Story of a Very Young Prisoner of Auschwitz
**Michael Bornstein and Debbie Bornstein Holinstat**

This memoir of a Jewish boy's survival in Auschwitz is written by Michael, who was 4 years old when the camp was liberated, with the help of his daughter Debbie. A gripping story, novelistically told, that is soothingly and sensitively written.

### Sachiko: A Nagasaki Bomb Survivor's Story
**Caren Stelson**

Sachiko Yasui was only 6 years old when the bomb fell on Nagasaki, killing her brother, her friends, and other family members. This extraordinary true account, told with immediacy and warmth, personalizes the terrors of atomic war and shows how people survive in the face of tragedy.

### Little Leaders: Bold Women in Black History
**Vashti Harrison**

One of many recent compendiums about the lives of inspiring women, this group biography is one of the best. Included among the forty women are well-known figures like Sojourner Truth and Harriet Tubman, but also less recognized figures, from athletes to military leaders. The illustrations are adorable, but the women depicted in the stories: amazing.

## YA

### The Queen of Katwe
**Tim Crothers**
The inspiring true story of a champion girl chess player who rises out of the slums of Uganda. This adult book, accessible for older teens, was also made into an excellent movie suitable for readers 13 and older.

### Brazen: Rebel Ladies Who Rocked the World
**Pénélope Bagieu**
A very cool graphic book from France: short, punchy, comics-style biographies of extraordinary women around the world who walked their own path and fought for what they believed in, from Tove Jansson, the creator of Moomins, to the astronaut Mae Jemison.

### I Am Malala
**Malala Yousafzai, with Christian Lamb**
Malala has become a Nobel Prize winner and international human rights icon since she wrote this searing memoir of her happy childhood, advocacy for girls' education, and attack by the Taliban. The incredible story still rings out in her clear, inspirational voice.

### Vincent and Theo: The Van Gogh Brothers
**Deborah Heiligman**
This sweeping, compassionate book explains the intertwined lives of the two Van Gogh brothers and their unusually powerful bond, drawing on the many letters Vincent wrote to Theo.

### Girl Rising: Changing the World One Girl at a Time
**Tanya Lee Stone**
A gorgeous, eye-opening, oversized book of photographs and stories about the international fight to give girls equal educational opportunities. It accompanies the documentary by the same name but more than stands on its own.

### Behind Rebel Lines: The Incredible Story of Emma Edmonds, Civil War Spy
**Seymour Reit**
One of those books that makes real history as thrilling as fiction: Cutting her hair and dressing in men's clothing, Emma Edmonds enlisted in the Union Army and became a bold, valuable spy behind Confederate lines.

### The March trilogy
**John Lewis and Andrew Aydin, illustrated by Nate Powell**
The civil rights movement is seen through the life story of Rep. Lewis in a powerful graphic tale that vibrates with drama, suspense, and the thrilling idea that young people can change the world.

### Boots on the Ground: America's War in Vietnam
**Elizabeth Partridge**
The Vietnam War was fought largely by teenagers or those who'd recently been teenagers—and the antiwar protests were often led by young people, too, as this photo-heavy book makes clear. It gives a good overview, driving home all that was at stake during the bitter war that drove the country apart.

## Drowned City: Hurricane Katrina & New Orleans
### Don Brown
A sobering and eye-opening graphic account of Katrina and its horrific aftermath, with an uplifting look at the heroism and courage of the many rescuers and helpers.

## Becoming Maria
### Sonia Manzano
Manzano was one of the first Latinas to break into mainstream TV, and her book is a beautifully written chronicle of an era and an exceptional life. We root for the charismatic Manzano as her acting talent develops in challenging childhood circumstances then soars in college and beyond.

## A Girl from Yamhill
### Beverly Cleary
This memoir by the beloved author of the Ramona and Henry Huggins books is a clear-eyed, unsentimental look at growing up in Oregon during the Great Depression as a girl from whom not much was expected. Fans will spot many episodes that later made their way into Cleary's iconic children's books.

# Science and Nature

## PICTURE BOOKS

## Locomotive
### Brian Floca
A real beauty and, like its subject, a marvel of ingenuity and invention. Intricately drawn and well-researched, this terrific Caldecott Medal–winning book on the history of trains shows how a great picture book can attract older readers as well as young. Other Floca greats: *Lightship*, on a kind of lighthouse-ship, and *Moonshot*, on space travel.

## Me . . . Jane
### Patrick McDonnell
One of the all-time best nonfiction picture books for young children, this biography of primatologist and activist Jane Goodall draws a simple but moving, sensitive portrait of the scientist as a young girl. The final spread is sure to provoke tears of astonishment and joy—at least among grown-up readers!

## Animals Upside Down
### Steve Jenkins and Robin Page
Steve Jenkins's books, often written with his wife, Robin Page, feature fascinating animal facts conveyed through distinct and arresting illustrations. Also highly recommended: *Eye to Eye*, *Creature Features*, and *Just a Second*.

## Life Story
### Virginia Lee Burton
One of the first picture books to portray evolution in all its majesty and wonder, this classic from 1962 has since been updated on the science. Most importantly, it gets the big picture right: showing young children how their own

lives fit into the grand tapestry of human existence and the universe. A wonder.

### Grand Canyon

**Jason Chin**

An outstanding visual and scientific introduction to one of the world's most majestic natural wonders. Everything an informational, nonfiction picture book should be, it includes a panoramic gatefold, maps, and other details for the obsessed.

### Owen & Mzee: The True Story of a Remarkable Friendship AND Cecil's Pride: The True Story of a Lion King

**The Hatkoff Family, with Dr. Paula Kahumbu, photographs by Peter Greste and Brent Stapelkamp**

These photographic picture books tell remarkable true stories of wild animal adaptation and resilience. Owen, a baby hippo orphaned by a 2004 tsunami, was adopted by Mzee, a 130-year-old giant tortoise. Cecil was the famous lion tragically killed by an American tourist; after his death, his former rival, Jericho, raised Cecil's cubs as his own.

### Neighborhood Sharks: Hunting with the Great Whites of California's Farallon Islands

**Katherine Roy**

This book not only showcases sharks but also offers a portrait of a wildlife refuge and the scientists whose life work is centered there. Roy did firsthand research, and it shows in her finely rendered artwork, in all its chilling terror and gore.

### Tiny Creatures: The World of Microbes

**Nicola Davies, illustrated by Emily Sutton**

We bet this is one your child will pore over for hours, read and reread, whether their initial response is "Cool" or "Yuck!" And it's about microbes! This imaginatively constructed book exemplifies the way smart science can be conveyed in creative and nontraditional ways. We suggest seeking out everything else by the wildly talented Davies.

### Over and Under the Snow

**Kate Messner, illustrated by Christopher Silas Neal**

Oh, the quiet beauty of nature! There's no better way to inspire awe than this meditative look at these parallel worlds. There's solid information, but the mood here is tranquility. *Over and Under the Pond* is a lovely follow-up by the same team.

### Snakes

**Nic Bishop**

Created by the master of children's nature-photography books, this one is a stunner, full of creepy photos for reptile fans. Bishop gets up close to give kids a visceral sense of the strange anatomy and terrifying behaviors of these often misunderstood creatures. Keep an eye out for other books with Bishop's remarkable photographs.

## A Hundred Billion Trillion Stars

Seth Fishman,
illustrated by Isabel Greenberg

Uses mind-boggling equations (seven billion people weigh about the same as ten quadrillion ants, for example) to lure even the most math-averse child. Math and space belong together in astrophysics; this book brings the two subjects together for younger minds in ways they can understand even as they shake their heads in awe.

# MIDDLE GRADE AND YA

### Bubonic Panic

Gail Jarrow

Yes, it's disgusting, and that's what makes it so fun. Fans of science, medicine, and outrageous facts will love the gross-out factor of this perfect nonfiction narrative step-up for *National Geographic* and Guinness World Record fact-obsessed readers. Also in this series, *Fatal Fever: Tracking Down Typhoid Mary*.

### The Impossible Rescue: The True Story of an Amazing Arctic Adventure

Martin W. Sandler

The riveting story of three men sent by President William McKinley over 1,500 miles of frigid Alaskan terrain to rescue whaling ships trapped in ice. This against-all-odds adventure is one of the great polar stories. Photographs and journal entries from one of the rescuers add to the thrill.

## The Way Things Work

David Macaulay

The coffee table–sized classic is constantly being updated, but it otherwise needs no improvement. Macaulay is the master of explaining intricate feats of engineering through detailed yet accessible drawings. From the simple zipper to the washing machine to the microprocessor, all become startlingly clear.

## Professor Astro Cat books

Dr. Dominic Walliman and Ben Newman

Why shouldn't cats teach science? Generously illustrated in a graphic, midcentury style with an impossibly cool cat at the center, these books by a quantum computer scientist break down scientific concepts into accessible components as they take kids on journeys through the wonders of space, atomic science, and the human body.

## Radioactive!: How Irène Curie and Lise Meitner Revolutionized Science and Changed the World

Winifred Conkling

Books about women scientists are all the rage; this latest addition, a dual biography, warrants being moved to the top of the stack. Neither woman got the recognition she deserved during her lifetime; both get it now.

### Science Comics

Various authors from First Second Books

Yes, that's the title of the series, and searching it or asking your librarian or bookseller for it will bring you to this group of colorful graphic nonfiction books that insert humor and narrative into child-friendly subjects. There's even the occasional cute factor. Best titles: *Volcanoes*, *Dogs*, and *Plagues*.

## Primates: The Fearless Science of Jane Goodall, Dian Fossey, and Biruté Galdikas
**Jim Ottaviani and Maris Wicks**
From the author of *Feynman* comes this accessible, smartly drawn, lightly fictionalized account of three giants of primatology. The graphic nonfiction three-part historical biography will inspire young scientists.

## Calling All Minds: How to Think and Create Like an Inventor
**Temple Grandin**
An inspirational guide from the famed scientist and inventor, who is also autistic. Filled with surprising facts and moving, personal stories, this is an impassioned plea to children urging them to see the world creatively and scientifically. They will.

## Charles Darwin's "On the Origin of Species": Young Readers Edition
**Adapted by Rebecca Stefoff**
This oversized adaptation of Charles Darwin's indispensable science classic is full of photos, scientific illustrations, and other appealing visuals, with the text made accessible, plus sidebars on topics such as modern misrepresentations of evolution.

## Blood, Bullets, and Bones: The Story of Forensic Science from Sherlock Holmes to DNA
**Bridget Heos**
With forensics newly popular among students and increasingly part of school curricula, this introduction is the high-quality nonfiction version of *CSI* for young minds.

## Something Rotten: A Fresh Look at Roadkill
**Heather L. Montgomery**
A wildlife researcher recounts her journey to discover more about not just the animals killed on our highways but the uses their corpses have been put to, scientific and otherwise. Fascinating and eye-opening, and the title is bound to catch even your most jaded reader's eye.

## Endangered, Threatened, Rescued, AND Orphaned
**Eliot Schrefer**
These books are fictional stories of bonobos, chimps, orangutans, and gorillas. As their thrilling stories unfold, they also deliver an unparalleled look at the world of primates and the threats they face from humans.

## Hidden Figures: Young Readers Edition
**Margot Lee Shetterly**
Adapted for teen readers, Shetterly's adult bestseller about the four African American women mathematicians at NASA who helped propel the space program in the face of both racial and gender prejudice will not fail to inspire and fascinate.

## Temple Grandin: How the Girl Who Loved Cows Embraced Autism and Changed the World
**Sy Montgomery**
This book goes inside the singular mind of the remarkable scientist, inventor, and advocate Grandin, showing how she made her breakthroughs and illuminating the challenges and opportunities that autism brings.

## Eyes Wide Open: Going Behind the Environmental Headlines
**Paul Fleischman**
Both a solid explanation of the urgent dangers facing our environment, and a useful guide to sorting through all the good and bad information about environmental threats and possible solutions.

# Historical Fiction

## PICTURE BOOKS

### Finding Winnie: The True Story of the World's Most Famous Bear
**Lindsay Mattick,**
**illustrated by Sophie Blackall**
This Caldecott Medal winner captures many dimensions of family connection through the generations, starting with a mom telling her boy a bedtime story about her own grandfather—who happened to be the soldier who tamed the real bear who became immortalized as Winnie-the-Pooh.

### Grandfather's Journey
**Allen Say**
One of the most poignant and memorable immigrant stories, this book recounts the life of Say's Japanese American grandfather, who was uprooted but always loved the two cultures he lived between. The art is stunning, and the story is emotional and universal.

### Leif the Lucky
**Ingri and Edgar Parin d'Aulaire**
This 1940s account of the transatlantic journey of Leif the Lucky, who was the son of Erik the Red and the first Nordic person to sail to America, reads like an adventure tale. The d'Aulaires' beautiful, timeless art makes you want to stop on each page even as the story hurtles you forward.

### Steamboat School
**Deborah Hopkinson,**
**illustrated by Ron Husband**
Little James and his family are free blacks in Missouri in 1840. When a state law is passed making education illegal for all blacks, his passionate teacher moves his school onto a steamboat on the Mississippi, leading James to appreciate the chance to learn as much as this book's young readers will.

### President Taft Is Stuck in the Bath
Mac Barnett,
illustrated by Chris Van Dusen
The legendary story of the rotund President Taft's bathtub mishap gets a hilarious telling. A delightful addition to more serious fare for kids fascinated with US presidents.

### The Potato King
Christoph Niemann
A playful glimpse at a fascinating bit of historical lore: how the clever Prussian king Frederick persuaded his reluctant people to eat potatoes. Niemann's delightful art is made partly with (of course) potato prints.

### The Gardener
Sarah Stewart,
illustrated by David Small
This moving story of the Depression is told through letters, with mesmerizing art. Lydia Grace must move away from her beloved garden to live with her baker uncle in the city, but she manages to transform the grim setting with the flowers she plants and an open heart.

### Oskar and the Eight Blessings
Richard Simon and Tanya Simon,
illustrated by Mark Siegel
A Hanukkah story and much more: Young Oskar arrives in New York City from Europe alone as the Holocaust is tearing apart his family. It's the first night of Hanukkah as well as Christmas Eve, and as he makes his way uptown to find his aunt, he's welcomed by big-hearted strangers.

### Queen Victoria's Bathing Machine
Gloria Whelan,
illustrated by Nancy Carpenter
How can Queen Victoria swim without her subjects glimpsing her in a bathing suit? In this witty rhyming tale based on a true story, Prince Albert comes to the rescue by inventing a contraption in which she can be wheeled down to the water.

### The Hawk of the Castle: A Story of Medieval Falconry
Danna Smith,
illustrated by Bagram Ibatoulline
This nifty book manages to convey the details of everyday family life in medieval England as well as the basics of falconry through the story of a girl whose father, the falcon master on a flourishing estate, teaches her his trade.

## CHAPTER BOOKS AND MIDDLE GRADE

### Esperanza Rising
Pam Muñoz Ryan
A well-off Mexican girl is forced to flee with her family to California and a hard life of farmwork in this novel set during the Great Depression. A lyrical, moving window into Western and labor history.

### Inside Out & Back Again
Thanhha Lai
A coming-of-age novel in verse inspired by Lai's own childhood as a refugee from Saigon after the Vietnam War. Lai's story of grief and accepting change is moving and unexpectedly funny.

## Breaking Stalin's Nose
**Eugene Yelchin**

Ten-year-old Sasha aspires to belong to the Soviet Young Pioneers, but when his father is arrested, his whole world is thrown into doubt. Yelchin's dramatic story of Soviet life is made even more memorable by his stunning charcoal drawings.

## The True Confessions of Charlotte Doyle
**Avi**

It's 1832, and 13-year-old Charlotte must return home to Rhode Island from England as the only female on a sinister ship with a mutinous crew. Thrills and suspense sit right alongside fascinating historical detail. Equally convincing is *Sophia's War: A Tale of the Revolution* by Avi.

## The War That Saved My Life
**Kimberly Brubaker Bradley**

A girl named Ada is kept inside by her mother because of her twisted foot, but when World War II breaks out, she sneaks away with her brother and is taken in by a kind woman who shows her how to live, even in dangerous times. Both suspenseful and sob-inducing, it was followed by an equally riveting sequel, *The War I Finally Won*, in which Ada faces a future full of surprising possibility.

## The Evolution of Calpurnia Tate
**Jacqueline Kelly**

Set at the turn of the twentieth century, this book introduces a sparky young heroine obsessed with the natural world and Darwin's still relatively new *On the Origin of Species*.

## Elijah of Buxton
**Christopher Paul Curtis**

Eleven-year-old Elijah, who lives in a settlement of runaway slaves in Canada, has to confront his own fears when he crosses the border to right a personal wrong. This vivid novel brims with Curtis's trademark humor and gift for capturing young people's voices.

## Number the Stars
**Lois Lowry**

The inimitable Lowry tells the story of a 10-year-old Danish girl who helps her family shelter the family of her Jewish best friend during the Holocaust. A devastating story balanced by its view into the heroism of the Danish resistance.

## The Wednesday Wars
**Gary D. Schmidt**

A Long Island teenager in 1968 has to navigate high school in the shadow of the Vietnam War. A subtle novel about finding your individual conscience in times of political unrest and social change.

## The Parker Inheritance
**Varian Johnson**

In an attic in South Carolina, a present-day girl finds letters from her grandmother that hint at a grave racial injustice decades ago, in the pre–civil rights era. She sets out to solve the mystery in this riveting novel, with twists and turns inspired by *The Westing Game*.

# YA

## Chains, Forge, AND Ashes (The Seeds of America trilogy)

**Laurie Halse Anderson**

Three enslaved teenage girls long for freedom during the Revolutionary War period in these richly researched and deeply moving books. The trilogy is a stunner and makes you wonder why there isn't more great narrative nonfiction about America's early days, especially for teenage readers. Also: Anderson's gripping account of yellow fever raging through Philadelphia, *Fever 1793*.

## Deadly

**Julie Chibbaro**

A medical thriller told in diary form, this imagined tale based on the real-life story of Mary Mallon, aka Typhoid Mary, centers on our diarist, Prudence Galewski, a 16-year-old Jewish tenement dweller who gets caught up in the mysterious ailment afflicting New York City. Combines highly engaging history with a heroine who cares more about scientific education than finishing school.

## Code Name Verity

**Elizabeth Wein**

Nazis, bombings, heart-pounding subterfuge. This historical novel beautifully captures the close friendship between two young women, a spy and a pilot, during World War II and is as sophisticated as any adult novel but intended for ambitious teenage readers. Not only great history but also one of the most astute depictions of true female friendship.

## Woods Runner

**Gary Paulsen**

We're in colonial America, on the cusp of war. Thirteen-year-old Samuel is a skilled hunter—a "woods runner"—from western Pennsylvania who must contend with British soldiers, Iroquois warriors, and Hessian mercenaries. The threats combine to make this vivid life of a teenager during wartime mesmerizing.

## What I Saw and How I Lied

**Judy Blundell**

This National Book Award winner by Blundell (prolific under the pseudonym Jude Watson) sets a love story in post–World War II Queens and Palm Beach, where 15-year-old Evie is figuring out her place in the world. Taut writing and great characters enhance this gripping story about lies, truth, and morality.

## Midwinterblood

**Marcus Sedgwick**

Sedgwick's books are always intricate, clever, and brain-twistingly good. This one encompasses seven love stories separated by centuries but mysteriously woven together. A vampire, a ghost, an airman, a Viking, a painter, and others figure into this challenging, provocative novel.

## Fatal Throne

**Candace Fleming, Linda Sue Park, M. T. Anderson, et al**

A killer lineup for this riveting, well-conceived book. Seven highly acclaimed authors take on the individual lives of Henry VIII and his six wives in seven chapters, each told in the first person. A gripping introduction to Tudor history, one that will surely leave your child ready for more. (If so, you can suggest Alison Weir's highly engaging history for grown-ups, *The Six Wives of Henry VIII*.)

### The Passion of Dolssa
**Julie Berry**
We're in Provensa (Provence) in 1241, in the aftermath of the Crusades. Dolssa de Stigata, an accused heretic, is close to death when Botille Flasucra tries to rescue her. This smart and lyrical story of faith, power, violence, and friendship, with a compelling, visionary teenage protagonist, will draw readers into an era not commonly covered by YA.

### The Conqueror's trilogy
**Kiersten White**
Like Game of Thrones set in Transylvania under the Ottoman Empire, this series is rife with betrayal, cunning, power grabs, fiendish plots, and intrigue. There's also romance. This is the kind of fare that will win dystopian thriller fans over to historical fiction.

### The Astonishing Life of Octavian Nothing, Traitor to the Nation
**M. T. Anderson**
Told in two volumes, this eye-opening story set during the Revolutionary War period concerns Octavian, who learns that he and others like him are slaves, unwittingly the subjects of medical experiments designed to prove the inferiority of certain races. A smart, literary take on a horrific subject. Also don't miss Anderson's fantastic hybrid illustrated collaboration with Eugene Yelchin, *The Assassination of Brangwain Spurge*, a political satire about an attempt at a truce between goblins and elves.

# Index

· · · · · · · · · ·

# Acknowledgments

We're hugely grateful to the incredible team at Workman, whose support and enthusiasm for this book has gone above and beyond: our dedicated editor, Mary Ellen O'Neill; Suzie Bolotin and Dan Reynolds; Janet Vicario; Traci Todd; Rebecca Carlisle, Chloe Puton, and Moira Kerrigan; Jessica Rozler; Laurel Robinson, Michael Ferut, Elizabeth Marotta, Kerianne Steinberg, and Barbara Stussy.

Our deepest thanks go to the four amazing illustrators who lent their talent: Dan Yaccarino, Vera Brosgol, Lisk Feng, and Monica Garwood, and to Jessica Hische for the knockout cover.

At the *Times*, heartfelt thanks to Karen Barrow, who conceived and edited the original "How to Raise a Reader" guide; Alex Ward; our stalwart colleagues on the Books Desk; Matt Dorfman; and Dean Baquet, the big boss.

To our agents, Lydia Wills and Sarah Burnes—thank you for everything.

And, of course, there is never enough gratitude for our patient families. Maria thanks Matt, Sketch, Gus, MJ, and Dante. Pamela thanks Michael, Beatrice, Tobias, and Teddy.